PRAYING WITH THE HEART OF THE CHURCH: LECTIONARY-BASED LECTIO DIVINA

Author:

Fr. David B. Rosenberg

Praying With the Heart of the Church: Lectionary-Based Lectio Divina

Cover photo credit: "God Alone at the Abbey of Gethsemani "; Photo by David B. Rosenberg 2011

First Printing: 2018

ISBN 978-1-365-75206-3

David B. Rosenberg
703 East Main Street
DeWitt, Michigan 48820

www.stfrancis.ws

Ordering Information:

Special discounts are available on quantity purchases by corporations, associations, educators, and others. For details, contact the publisher at the above listed address.

U.S. trade bookstores and wholesalers: Please contact Saint Francis Retreat Publications Tel: (517) 669-8321; email: bookstore@stfrancis.ws

20180804

Dedication

Cor ad Cor Loquitur
Heart speaks to Heart

I dedicate this book to Christian Pilgrims everywhere. May your journey on the Way of the Cross bring you spiritual growth, consolations, and a compassionate heart.
May you be "Joyous Ones"!

Watch, O Lord,
with those who wake,
or watch, or weep tonight,
and give Your angels and saints
charge over those who sleep.
Tend your sick ones, O Lord Christ.
Rest Your weary ones.
Bless Your dying ones.
Soothe Your suffering ones.
Pity your afflicted ones.
SHIELD YOUR JOYOUS ONES,
and all for Your love's sake. Amen.
(Prayer of St. Augustine)

Contents

Acknowledgements

I would like to thank the Lay Directors, Presenters and Facilitators at the St. Francis Retreat Center in DeWitt Michigan; my professors and mentors and my family without whose help this book would never have been completed.

Fr. Charlie, thank you for writing the foreword.

I especially thank the saints whose life works illuminated the Church with wisdom and guidance.

Foreword

Delight in the Gift!

Praying is more than the mere recitation of words. Praying is not passive. It is an activity that leads us to act, to do what the Divine would guide us to do. Praying does not put God at our disposal; it puts us at the disposal of God.

Contrary to the voices which surround us in our fractured culture, our souls are saved in active belonging. We do not save ourselves, God saves us. We do not justify ourselves, God justifies us. Paradoxically we are saved by intentionally belonging.

We enter a church that pre-exists us. We enter a church -- a community of faith-filled believers -- given to us by God. Our participation in the community we call Church is realized and activated by us as individuals. Religion is corporate as well as individual. We are sponsored into it. God is OUR Father, not just my Father.

Participating in the life of the church requires that we do so reflectively and intentionally, not mindlessly or merely passively. To be sure, the church acts for us and upon us but it does so only by our free and intentional choice.

Prayer is our invitation that asks the Holy Spirit to act upon us and act within us. Inspiration -- *"in-spirit-ization"* -- is the result. Praying turns off the noise of this world that deafens us. Praying clears away the clutter of this world so that we might hear the quiet whisperings of the Holy Spirit who sings His love song to our souls. Praying *"spiritizes"* us. It sensitizes us and allows us to be at the disposal of God.

Spiritual directors and guides are sometimes asked: "What should I do when I pray?" The answer -- Just make yourself available to God.

Give God your eyes to see and ears to hear. *Reflect!* Reflection is the key to it all. It's all about letting God take you by the hand so that He might show you things.

The gift of Fr. Rosenberg is that he has not given us a "How to" book so much as a book that gives us a vision of what we are doing when we pray. Better said, it is a book about what we are doing and what the Holy Spirit is doing. When we stand back and see the basic dynamic in our relationship with our Father, we see that God offers and we respond. God gives us the gift and we open it. Nothing happens unless and until we open it.

Delight in the Gift!

Rev. Fr. Charles Irvin
Founding Editor,
Faith Magazine
Diocese of Lansing

Preface

Why might this book be for *you*? Why Lectio Divina? Most Catholics ask the question the disciples asked Jesus, *"Lord, Teach us to pray"*. (see Luke 11:1). First, this book will help you connect to the mind of the Church through its annual calendar of readings. Second, it offers a path to embrace the heart of the church in your prayer life. Together these two ancient practices are made accessible for us living in the Third Millennium.

The first practice follows the Sunday Lectionary of the Mass which guides us to "Praying with the Heart of the Church." In its simplest form, we follow the Sunday Mass Readings through the liturgical Church Calendar.

The Roman Catholic Liturgical Calendar

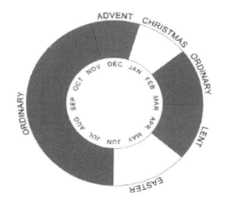

When we look at the Sunday Gospel readings within the Church calendar, we see that Mother Church in her wisdom "feeds" us scripture as lessons from the School of Jesus. The purpose is to shape our hearts and minds to the natural rhythm of the Church Year with the desire to lead us to wisdom and holiness. In an annual cycle these weekly liturgical lessons follow the cadence of the Church's calendar year, beginning with Advent in late November or early December.

We move from Advent Season to Christmas Season, Ordinary Time, Lent, Triduum in Holy Week, Easter Season, then back to Ordinary Time, returning once again to Advent, the beginning of our year.

Roman Catholic Church Lectionary for the Sunday Mass

The word lectionary simply means "readings," for us a collection of selected readings from scripture. These Readings are designed to take us on a pilgrim's journey across Salvation History, which begins with the Old Testament Book of Genesis. It then travels across the ages of the Salvation History of the Chosen People; up to the New Testament chronicle of the ministry of John the Baptist. It continues with the life, passion, death, resurrection and ascension of our Savior Jesus Christ. It culminates with the early Church's witness to the power of the Risen Christ through the love of the Father and the grace of the Holy Spirit. The Solemnity of Our Lord Jesus Christ, King of the Universe wraps up the Lectionary calendar year. We hear the joyful pleas of the disciples as they push onward toward the New Jerusalem crying out, "Marana, Tha! -- Come, Lord Jesus!" - the closing two words in the Book of Revelation that concludes the beautiful and diverse sacred collection of writings we call the Bible.

The Sunday Lectionary is organized in a three-year cycle (Cycle A, B, and C.) This order came about following the Second Vatican Council, which called Catholics, through the Sunday readings at Mass, to become more familiar with the text of the Bible. As a result we now have a three-year cycle of readings built around readings from the three synoptic[i] Gospels of Matthew, Mark, and Luke, and interspersed throughout with the Gospel of John. The deeper practice is Lectio Divina (Latin for "Divine Reading") which takes on a spiritual dimension. This book offers a practical guide for all Christians to bring these two practices into their everyday life, building a lifetime rule for discipleship on a pilgrim's journey to the New Jerusalem.

Introduction

"Let the word of Christ dwell in you richly, as in all wisdom you teach and admonish one another, singing psalms, hymns, and spiritual songs with gratitude in your hearts to God. And whatever you do, in word or in deed, do everything in the name of the Lord Jesus, giving thanks to God the Father through him." (Colossians 3:16-17)

We are called regularly to an "experience of desert" seeking silence and solitude, as our Desert Fathers did in the Early Church. It is here that we come to recognize more clearly and truly who God is, who we are, who others are, what the world is, and the reality of grace versus evil. We try to clarify God's view of us – creatures with such a special destiny. We come to more perfectly view ourselves as persons made in the image of God. Through this discovery, we see our need for God and appreciate the extent to which the likeness has been lost, and is recovered through Jesus Christ. With the Practice of Lectio Divina we seek to deepen our interpersonal relationship with God through reflection, prayer and contemplation. We are ultimately called to respond in action to what has been gained through our practice of Lectio Divina.

There is a wise saying attributed to St. Pachomius (b.292), a Desert Father from the third century:

Here is the monk's life-work, holy obedience, meditation, prayer, not judging others, not complaining. For it is written: "Let those who love the Lord hate evil, for he guards the lives of his faithful ones and delivers them from the hand of the wicked." (Psalm 97:10) This is the monk's life. Not to walk in agreement with an unjust man, nor to look with the eyes upon evil, nor to go about being lustful and curious, and neither to examine nor listen to the business of others. Never take without properly and gratefully receiving, and give to others. Not to be proud of heart, nor to malign others in one's thoughts. Not to fill the stomach, but in all things to behave with discretion. Behold, in all this you have the heart and soul of a monk.

As we see here, the wisdom and times of the early Desert Fathers in the fourth century gave us this gift, that of striving for holy obedience, meditation, prayer, and not judging others. These were the spiritual practices, you might say spiritual seeds, that sprang up in the desert from the waters of the eternal Rivers of living water. "Let anyone who thirsts come to me and drink. Whoever believes in me, as scripture says 'Rivers of living water will flow from within him.'" (John 7:37-38)

The human heart desires to drink deeply from this living water. It's no small wonder these practices were so widely desired in the Early Church. In every generation we are urged to find such a path. Sacred Scripture, the sayings of the Wisdom Folk, the sanctuary of solitude for extended meditation and reflection, and from this, the font of love flowing from us to the world.

We begin with a "Grow and Go Quick Start Guide" to give you a taste of this ancient practice called Lectio Divina. If you hunger for more, we offer you an exploration of the method Guigo the Carthusian, followed by the Spanish Mystics of the sixteenth century: the Carmelites and Jesuits; then the insights of the theologians that influence of Vatican II. Finally, we enter the Third Millennium and the inspiring words of Pope Benedict from his document in 2010, "Verbum Domini -- The God Who Speaks" in which he profoundly posits, "If [Lectio Divina] is effectively promoted, this practice will bring to the Church — I am convinced of it — a new spiritual springtime."

May Our Lord bless you with "a new spiritual springtime," as you compose your thoughts and spend some time praying with the heart of the Church.

Lesson 1
Grow and Go Quick Start Guide

I noticed some years ago that user manuals packed in the boxes of new computers, printers, user software and electronics in general started getting thinner and smaller. This was in response to our shortened attention spans. In place of thick instructions that we no longer had the patience to tediously wade through, we got "Quick Start Guides." One such guide might read, *"Follow these 5 easy steps, and you'll be on your way in no time!"* Your imaginary conversation with the manufacturer might go something like this: *"Give me some short steps so I can get this thing "booted up," I'll take it for a "test drive," then I can decide if I like it enough to 'look under the hood' and see how this modern marvel is put together."* In writing this book, I kept coming back to this simple reality. If we are going to make a major investment in time, we want to first know it's going to be worth it. A lot of us seem to all want *"quick start guides,"* not only with our electronic stuff, but with the rest of our lives, as well.

Using this concept, I considered the potential audience for this book. Like me, might they want to *"jump start"* this experience? Then, if the *"test drive"* feels right, they'll likely want to *"look under the hood"* at things like the historical origins, and theory. Hence, the title to this lesson, the purpose of which is to get you on your way.

Lectio Divina

Lectio:	The Art of Listening
Meditatio:	The Art of Reflection
Oratio:	The Art of Prayer from a Grateful Heart
Contemplatio:	The Art of Self-Emptying
Operatio:	The Art of Ministry
	Grow: Spiritual Maturity
	Go: ...to the Mission Field

Lectio Divina – The Art of Living Sacred Scripture
First Movement, the Art of Active Listening

"Be still, and know that I am God." Psalm 46:10

The first movement is Lectio, the Art of Active Listening. The transmission of the Gospel message, through reading or hearing, or even Braille, to the physical senses of the topic requires active listening. If the physical senses are impeded, we cannot move forward.

Before we get too far into our Quick Start Guide, let's start with a modern story, a simple allegory that you might well identify with, that gets to the heart of the first three movements: the Reading, Reflection and Prayer of Lectio Divina. Each movement is progressive, and very much interdependent on each other. I call this "Joe's Story"

Joe's Story

Have you ever been lost in an unknown place, driving in a seemingly aimless fashion, looking for some way to get a decent set of directions? Our main character, Joe, has found himself in just such a predicament. He is to be the Best Man for his good friend's wedding today, which is to take place in a small chapel, in a rural, picturesque village in New England with its uneven landscape and twisted, turning roads. Driving off with his Smartphone on the roof of his car, his spirits sank as he realized he had no GPS and no way to call for help. Then, as he got out of the metropolitan area he hit a dense fog. This cost him considerable time, and that comfortable padding which he had calculated would get him easily to the chapel on time. But now he's lost, feeling anxious and concerned. And low on gas.

Finally seeing a gas station ahead, he pulls in, and looks for someone to ask directions. Unfortunately, the only person around is a scruffy old man, in seedy clothes and a coat buttoned to his chin, pumping gas into an old, beat up Ford Fiesta. Not your first choice to ask directions from. But Joe had no other options.

Taking a chance, Joe approached and asked the man if he knew how to get to the chapel, explaining how he came to be nearly late and quite frantic. As it turned out, this man looked up at Joe with surprisingly clear eyes, proceeded to tell him clearly and concisely how to get to the chapel. Joe, listening intently because he really had no choice, and quite taken aback by the lucidity of the man, got the message. The man finishes and Joe looks at him, and responds with a simple, "OH, I SEE!"

There are a few interesting points here from our perspective as observers. First, it took a crisis for Joe to go where common sense would advise him not to. Putting his ego aside, he humbled himself to ask for directions from a questionable source. But he was, after all, in a tight spot. In Joe's mind, it was a happy coincidence to cross paths with the man at all. More importantly to the point of Lectio, Joe was forced to stand still and actively listen, absorbing what the man had to say.

But the most interesting point to us the observer was his statement, "OH, I SEE!" Joe didn't actually "see" a map. He "heard" a map. Through intentional active listening, his mental faculty transformed what he heard through his physical ear, to "seeing" with his mental eye. That process "drew" the map on his mental screen. We do this type of physical to mental translating all the time. We just don't give it much thought.

I would like you to think about this sensorial translation process. How many senses do we have? Most say we have five. Some say we also have a sixth sense. But I suggest to you that we have fifteen senses on three plains of human existence: five physical, five mental, and five spiritual senses.

The Spiritual Director in me would say the Holy Spirit took advantage of Joe's Crisis. Joe has a good life, not many let downs, so for the first time in memory, he felt a growing sense of desolation. I say it was providential, not coincidental, that he was led to the "scruffy old" man. Providence gave him little choice but to experience the Lectio art of active listening, which requires the use of the first two plains of existence, physical and mental. This is not so easy in the context of our modern culture where we typically have shortened attention spans, usually of under a minute. Learning the new habit of active listening takes time. Plan on taking up to forty days to move from cultural restlessness to the calmness that affords us the luxury of the several minutes it takes to move through the Liturgy of the Word at Mass, or, in Joe's case, patiently and actively listening to directions.

Meditatio: The Art of Reflection

At this point, Joe, ever pragmatic, could simply have jumped in his car, laid rubber in the parking lot, and sped away toward his destination. That is what many would do. The last thing they have time for is to *reflect* on the experience. But Joe just had a brush with the consequences of ruining a bride's day. Instead of rushing off, he sat back for a moment, as he reflected on this "ah ha" God moment. He realized that if it wasn't for that scruffy man, he might well be facing the wrath of a bedeviled bridal party.

Joe, feeling guilty for not even thanking the man for his help, thought for a moment how he would feel if the tables were turned. Then he remembered his own aging grandparents, and how long it had been since he had taken a moment to call them. They had been so supportive of him during some difficult and rebellious teen years, challenges with school, and arguments with his parents. What had become of the loving child he once was?

Oratio: The Art of Prayer from a Grateful Heart

Joe got out of the car, went back to the man, and thanked him. A compassionate heart had overcome Joe. Joe felt the urge to pay for the man's gas. The man simply said, "Thank you, son. Blessed be God, in his goodness, forever."

He returned to the car feeling a surge of gratitude for a blessed life. For just a moment, he closed his eyes, breathed deeply of this renewed life, and said, "Lord, thank you for giving me this day!"

This surge of gratitude to God, bubbling from the wellspring of life, is the simplest yet most powerful form of prayer. Prayer from a grateful heart is the best gift anyone can offer to God.

Taking Lectio Divina for a Test Drive

This book documents a path to ongoing transformation through Lectionary-Based Lectio Divina, the breaking open of the upcoming Sunday scripture readings, both individually and in a small group setting.

1. The Art of Active Listening: Lectio

Small Group Setting:

To start, I suggest bringing together a small group of no less than three and no more than six people. This can be a combination of family and friends. It might even be just your spouse or a best friend. Whatever you see as the best way to "test the water." Have your bible with you.

- o Begin with a group prayer, such as.

> *"Come Holy Spirit, fill the hearts of your faithful and kindle in us the fire of your love. Send forth your Spirit and we shall be created. And You shall renew the face of the earth."*

> *Lord, send us your spirit, as we relax our minds, hearts and bodies, to prepare ourselves to receive wisdom from your Sacred Scripture.*

- o The first time you meet, read the first part of Joe's Story, "The Art of Active Listening," and have the group consider intentionally practicing this skill.
- o Have the group open their bibles to the Gospel of Luke, chapter 4, verses 16 through 21 (Luke 4:16-21).
- o Select one person from the group to read this aloud:

(Luke 4:16-21)
Jesus came to Nazareth, where he had grown up, and went according to his custom into the synagogue on the Sabbath day. He stood up to read and was handed a scroll of the prophet Isaiah. He unrolled the scroll and found the passage where it was written:

"The Spirit of the Lord is upon me,
because he has anointed me
to bring glad tidings to the poor.
He has sent me to proclaim liberty to captives
and recovery of sight to the blind,
to let the oppressed go free,
and to proclaim a year acceptable to the Lord."

Rolling up the scroll, he handed it back to the attendant and sat down, and the eyes of all in the synagogue looked intently at him.

He said to them, *"Today this scripture passage is fulfilled in your hearing."*

2. The Art of Reflection: Spending time with Meditatio

Following the reading, the leader then reads the second part of Joe's Story, Meditatio: The Art of Reflection. After reading it, have the group consider this movement. Then take a few minutes for silent reflection. The leader of the group then rereads the passage one more time. This time everyone except the reader is asked close their eyes, and listen for one particular verse that stands out, a verse that breathes a new kind of life into the heart. Holding on to that verse, reflect on it for a few moments, spending time in silence and reflection.

Did a particular verse speak to you? For me this time it was, *The Spirit of the Lord is upon me.* We just finished praying the Holy Spirit Prayer. That's exactly what we asked for, for the Spirit of the Lord to come upon us. What does that mean? For me, I felt an emotional response. I feel a calming yet joyful presence hovering about me, surrounding me, protecting me. Changing me! I am loved. I feel empowered, and I feel a strong desire to react to this love.

3. The Art of Prayer from a Grateful Heart: Oratio

Read the final section of Joe's Story, "Oratio: The Art of Prayer from a Grateful Heart." Think about his story in the context of your story. Hopefully you were moved to feel grateful for having a breath-catching response to hearing the scripture, as if for the first time. This is a heartfelt response to *reflecting* on one small verse that catches your attention. A response of gratitude to Our Lord should rise naturally from the fount of your joyful heart. This sense of gratitude that follows reflection is the most profound yet simple form of prayer.

> *Give me a pure heart that I may see thee,*
> *A humble heart that I may hear thee,*
> *A heart of love that I may serve thee,*
> *A heart of faith that I may abide in thee,*
> *Dear lord, give me a new heart.*
>
> *Fr David*

Most of us, when we start our Lectio Divina journey, believe we have trouble knowing how to pray. But, when gratitude is a response to God for this gift of scripture, that gratitude rises like incense to our Lord, and IS the ultimate prayer, that profound dialog with God.

Lesson 2
Overview: the Classic Approach

At The Wellsprings of Prayer

'Seek and you shall find.
Knock and the door will be opened for you.' (Matt 7:7-8)

The Holy Spirit is the living water "welling up to eternal life" in the heart that prays. It is he who teaches us to accept it at its source: Christ. Indeed in the Christian life there are several wellsprings where Christ waits to enable us to drink of the Holy Spirit.

The Church "forcefully and specially exhorts all the Christian faithful... to learn 'the surpassing knowledge of Jesus Christ' (Phil 3:8) by frequent reading of the divine Scriptures. In the Christian life, we are called to spiritually develop and grow. Lectio Divina, in its best practice, uses a model of three legs of a tripod of Christian development, piety, study, and action. Using this model, we are called to not only read scripture, but also to pray, so that a dialogue can take place between God and man. We speak to him when we pray. We listen to him when we read his inspired Word, and then we act on what inspires us, going out into the world with Christ's merciful love.

Thy word is a lamp unto my feet, and a light unto my path. (Psalm 119:105)

Historical Origins of Lectio Divina
The earliest documented accounts of Lectio Divina were composed by a monk, Guigo the Carthusian, living in the 12th century in what is now modern day France. Guigo the Carthusian is a wonderful teacher for those desiring to grow spiritually. He refers us to Matthew 7:7, summarizing the dispositions of the heart that is nourished by the word of God in prayer *"Seek in reading and you will find in meditating; knock in mental prayer and it will be opened to you by contemplation."*ii He described the stages which he saw as essential to the practice of Lectio Divina.

Although today you will see the expression "Lectio Divina" to mean many things, from simply reading scripture to structuring it around individual or small group prayer time, Guigo understood it to be much more. Over his lifetime he developed a system and method which, fortunately for all who came after him, was well documented. His method became the foundation for many spiritualities and a rules of life. This book will cover the significant historical movements and trends in this book, such as the Carmelite and Ignatian Lectio Divina practices, and from modern times, the method practiced by Thelma Hall, R.C. Over the centuries Guigo's formula was viewed as fundamental to most, if not all, Lectio Divina spiritual practices.

The Carthusian Way: Contemplation

The goal of the Carthusian Way is contemplation by the power of the Holy Spirit, living as unceasingly as possible in the light of the love of God made manifest in Christ.

"Blessed are the pure in heart, for they shall see God." (Mt 5:8)

When we seek purity of heart we are emptied of all but Christ's divine mercy, which right orders our lives to pour out that mercy and love to others. This also becomes threaded within the very fabric of our day through our works and actions. St. Benedict called this *"Ora et Labora"* -- *"Piety through Works"* -- pure and continuous prayer through the work of our hands.

Guigo learned through the teachings of St Bruno, founder of the Carthusians, that the fruits of contemplation are liberty, peace, and joy. *"O Bonitas! O Goodness!"* This is the cry that poured forth from the heart of St. Bruno, but the unification of the heart and the entrance into contemplative rest constitutes a long journey.

For Guigo this goal of contemplation would be a journey of the heart; a journey that would take many years of sacrifice, hard toil, ceaseless prayer, and holy imagination.

Imagine the lifestyle of that era, a lifestyle of ascetic practices by many Christians in the hope of spiritual union with God. This compelled Guigo to enter the monastery at a very young age. Guigo was but a man-child, yet large and muscular of frame. For him labor came easily, especially holy labor done for God's Glory. His daily prayer was for God to use the fruit of his labor to add beauty to God's plan, or "*Opus Dei*" the "*Work of God.*"

For Guigo, given his large stature, and coming from a well-to-do family, his greatest challenge and sacrifice was the strict ascetic practice of fasting. The largely vegetarian diet of the monastery was a daily routine of simple bread and water, supplemented with vegetables grown in their gardens. The Sabbath feast on Sunday was the biggest meal of the week. In keeping with the Lord's commandment to keep holy the Sabbath the monks shared the Eucharistic Banquet in the morning, followed by the Sabbath Feast and rest from all labor.

Guigo's two great pleasures in life became feasting on the Sunday Gospel and the Sabbath Banquet. Through fasting and contemplation, the two pleasures became synonymous. In his very active imagination, by Monday he could smell the faintest of aromas that would become his Sunday feast. The scent grew stronger day by day as did his hunger from his hard labor in the fields with only meager sustenance. In his daydreams, he would also imagine the pure joy of taking in the Sunday Gospel, being near Jesus as he taught, consoled, healed and forgave sins. Day by day his desire for Jesus' Sunday lesson grew. He felt an ever increasing spiritual hunger that drew him with cords of love to Jesus his Lord and Savior.

Part I
Guigo's Ladder of Monks

Lectio Divina

Lectio:　　　　Like taking a bite of solid food

Meditatio:　　Like chewing the food

Oratio:　　　　Like savoring the taste in gratitude

Contemplatio: Like enjoying the nourishment

By the time Guigo, died in 1188, he left two significant manuscripts behind entitled the Ladder of Monks and Meditations. It was in the Ladder of Monks that Guigo synthesized his system of the four movements of Lectio Divina. Earlier we discussed how he compared the movements to rungs of a ladder, and to the pleasure of dining:

1. Reading Scripture (Lectio), the first rung is like taking solid food in the mouth as we carefully study the Scriptures, and concentrate our powers on it.

2. Reflecting on the meaning (Meditatio), the second rung is like chewing food ingested by the mouth. It is the busy application of the mind to seek the help of one's own reason for knowledge of hidden truth.

3. Responding through prayer (Oratio), the third rung is like savoring the flavor of food. It is the heart's devoted turning to God in gratitude ("Barakah[iii]") for all that is gift, for all that is good.

4. Resting in the Sacred Heart of Jesus (Contemplatio), the fourth rung is like enjoying the nourishment of the food. It is when the mind is lifted up to God and held above itself, so that it enjoys the nourishment of the everlasting sweetness of resting within the Sacred Heart of Jesus.

As we break open Guigo's little manuscript on the Monks Ladder, we paint quite a picture of how our Lord, through the Holy Spirit, worked to bring Guigo's manual labor, and his passion for Holy Scripture to build Guigo's beautiful opus.

For the remainder of the chapter, I've included a significant portion of Guigo's ancient yet beautiful writings.

A Ladder of Four Rungs
By Which We May Well Climb To Heaven

Guigo, so legend tells, was hard at work one day, thinking about the spiritual work needed for God's servants. For him, four spiritual works came to mind: **reading, reflection, prayer** and **contemplation**. Like a ladder for all God's beloved children, we can climb from earth to heaven. It is a marvelously tall ladder, but with just four rungs, the one end standing on the ground, the other piercing through the clouds, revealing to the climber heavenly secrets.

This is the ladder Jacob saw in Genesis (Genesis 28:12), standing on the earth and reaching into heaven, on which he saw heavenly angels ascending and descending, with God supporting the ladder. The angels descend to delight us with spiritual consolation, and return to carry our prayers up to our Lord in heaven, where he sits on high, returning yet again to quench the desires of our heart. This idea is best quoted by St Augustine in his book "Confessions": 'You have made us for Yourself, oh God, and our hearts are restless until they find rest in You.' God supports the ladder, always ready to help his children climb the four rungs of this ladder, who neither fear nor doubt that such a ladder will really help.

Let's look closely at each of the four rungs of this ladder:

Reading: Actively hearing God's Word in Holy Scripture with full active participation.

Reflecting: Searching the inner self to reveal what was before concealed through spiritual blindness.

Praying: Once we understand what was once hidden, our heart cannot but help express gratitude for being able to at last grasp what is good and avoid what is evil.

Contemplation: The lifting up of the heart to God, tasting some of the heavenly sweetness.

Reading seeks
Reflecting finds
Praying gives back
Contemplation feels

Seek through reading, and you will find holy reflection and meditation in your thinking; knock through praying, and the door shall be opened to you to enter through heavenly contemplation to feel what you desire.

Reading is the first rung that precedes and leads us into meditation. It is like putting whole food into your mouth. It is like the outer shell of a delicious nut.

Reflection and meditation, the second rung, is like the meat of the nut. We earnestly seek, dig and dive deeply to find that treasure, and because we cannot attain this alone, God sends us into deep prayer.

The third rung, prayer is the natural expression of gratitude in response to what we have been given. Prayer rises to God, where we find the sweetness and delight of contemplation, that treasure we so fervently desire.

Guigo's fourth rung, contemplation is in the delight of the great sweetness of the gift. When contemplation comes, it yields the harvest of the labor of the other three through sweet, heavenly dew that the soul drinks in delight and joy.

The first rung is for beginners, the second for those rising from it, the third for those who are devout, the fourth for those who are holy and blessed of God. The four rungs are so bound together, and each of them so supporting each other, that the first two, reading and reflection, only help a little or not all, without the prayer and contemplation that follow. Without the first two we cannot realize the last two. What use is it to spend your time reading or listening to the deeds of the Holy Fathers, unless we "bite" and "chew" on those words through reflection, where we draw out the rich spiritual nourishment and send it to the heart. Through this action we may find and understand our own faults, and after this discovery, set ourselves to work in the hope that we may attain the graces of those virtues nested within them. Guigo has more to say about grace later in this chapter.

How the Four Rungs Are Closely Joined Together

It is the will of God for us to pray for this blessed grace, and open our heart when he comes, and assent with our free will to receive his grace. This is the consent Christ Jesus asked of the Samaritan woman to whom he spoke at the well, as she stood there to draw water: 'Go, and call your husband', as if to say, 'I will give you my grace if you ask for it.' He asked her to pray when he said, 'If you knew God's gift, and who he is who says to you "Give me drink", perhaps you would ask him and he would give you living water'.

When the woman heard Jesus' words, she thought in her heart that it was good and necessary to drink of this precious living water of which Christ spoke. Immediately with great desire she prayed to have this water and said, 'Lord, give me this water'. See how hearing of Christ's word and following that meditation with deep thought in her heart moved her to pray for this water. How else could she have been so moved to pray unless desire sprang from her heart like living water? What could she possibly otherwise have thought such a reflection would offer? To have your reflections richly rewarded you must pray with devotion, then you might be blessed with the sweetness of contemplation.

Reading without meditation is idle, reflection without prayer is without effect, but prayer with devotion leads to blessed contemplation. To ascend to the high ladder of contemplation without prayer, would be miraculous. The power of Almighty God is endless, and his mercy above all his works. We should do what we must - read and set our hearts deeply on God's holy law, and heartily pray that he give us strength in our weakness, and pours out his mercy to forgive our wretchedness. We must ever lean on him with love, making our cry to him, for from the blessed Lord is the cure for our souls. As Peter said, 'Stand firm with holy love after my grace, and you shall have what you desire. This is the grace we must win with endurance and strength.' These are the four rungs of this wonderful ladder.

Blessed be all who leave vanities and spend their time in holy counsel, and those that sell all and buy the field in which lies the surpassing treasure of sweetness. As our Lord says, 'See how sweet God our Savior is.' We ascend this ladder degree to degree, from stair to stair, and from virtue to virtue, until we see the God of gods in Zion, in the bliss of heaven.

The First and Second Rungs: Reading And Reflecting

Christ says in the Gospel of Matthew, "Blessed are the pure in heart, for they will see God." *Matt 5:8.* This passage, though simple sounding is full of the virtue of goodness and sweetness, and when lived out in our Christian life has a great effect, and paves the way for a rewarding life. When we hear this verse with our physical senses, and let it settle into the ears of our heart we see the impact of this virtue clearly as Jesus speaks to our soul and says, 'This verse may be lifted as on eagles wings and make its way to Abba your heavenly father. Seek his guidance from the depths of your heart, and through his graces be of pure heart. What a rich gift this is, to be rewarded with a taste of the bliss of heaven. Christ himself promises us that we shall see God, a sight that is the fulfillment of all desire and a joy for all who are friends of God.'

When we hear or read this lesson, 'Blessed are the pure of heart for they shall see God,' we begin as if to chew it and break it open with mind and reason. We yearn to attain this cleanness that is so precious and so mighty that it illuminates the hearts of those who have it that they might see God.

Through reflection and meditation we go and search. Christ taught us that it is soul cleansing that illuminates the pathway to holiness, not ritual bodily cleansing. I would remind you of what David the psalmist asks in Psalm 23, ' The LORD is my shepherd; there is nothing I lack. In green pastures he makes me lie down; to still waters he leads me; he restores my soul. He guides me along right paths for the sake of his name.' There it is immediately answered, *Even though I walk through the valley of the shadow of death, I will fear no evil, for you are with me; your rod and your staff comfort me. (Psalm 23)*

Who shall climb or ascend into the hill of God in heaven? Who shall stand in that holy place, there to see God in the beatific vision? The Holy Spirit through David answers us, 'Those who do no evil and whose hearts are clean within'. In meditation we think deeply how the same Prophet David fervently prayed for this cleanness, *'Create in me a clean heart...'* We know that if there is wickedness in our hearts, our inner voice to God is muted. We think about the holy man, Job, how fearful he was that he was not filled with foul thought when he said, 'I have made a covenant with my eyes that I should not think of a woman or of a virgin'. How strictly that holy man restrained himself shutting his eyes against vanities, not casting his eyes unwisely on the thing that might cause a loss of chastity. His path is then cleared to a pure heart.

As we become aware that through vanity we again becomes unclean, we begin to taste the delectable, joyful consolation, and see the glorious face of Jesus Christ, the font of all that is good, gracious and lovely, crowned with all joy, clothed with all bliss, as his Father clothed him at his Resurrection. It is within this golden sight we find the perfection of joy, of which the prophet spoke, 'Lord, when you show your glorious face to me I shall be fulfilled.' Once he sees that so much sweetness comes from so few words, the fire is kindled from so small a spark. With joy he shouts, 'Blessed be the clean of heart!' He beats the shimmering scroll out of the blazing fire, and draws it out in length and breadth.

When the soul of a glowing brand of this fire is enflamed and so ravished in desire to that thing that is the true reward of a clean heart, and for a moment gets to glance at the backside of God, then, like an alabaster box of sweet ointment begins to break, sweet smells come forth. With smelling not tasting, one understands the sweet flavor, and then joyfully tastes the sweetness. Truly, seek and you shall find, and indeed the shimmering pearl beyond all price is indeed discovered in the seeking.

But what of those of us who so desire to feel this delight, only to find it is just beyond our grasp. For the tighter we hold on to this, the more sorrow we find, because we cannot find the sweetness of the clean of heart. Meditation shows, but does not give, for neither through reading nor through reflection can we come to this sense of sweetness, but only through the gift that comes from above. In a mysterious way, to always be reading and reflecting is the blessing and the curse common to both good and evil: for the philosophers through exercise of their reason found but a sliver of the goodness of God. Because they did not know God and his goodness, nor loved him, nor worshipped him as God, were never consoled with the sweetness and liking of God that can only come through the gift of blessed wisdom, and therefore God withheld it from them for they were unworthy. It was like a golden scroll turned to dust and sifted through the fingers. It all disappeared into nothing. Study alone does not give us the spirit of wisdom, the spiritual gives wisdom and rich flavor to the soul when it comes, and stirs us with spiritual joy. Only this is spiritual joy and the gift of God and his teaching to his chosen disciples. This wisdom is gained by nothing but grace that comes from above. To this wisdom we must open not the ear but the heart. This wisdom is hidden from learned men of the world, but shown and opened to the lowly and meek, to fully understand and feel.

Strength rises from humility where neither tongue nor ear gains intelligence. God keeps wisdom for his chosen, that all may know and understand there is a Master in heaven, who teaches true wisdom and learning through his grace. He enlightens his chosen and helps them know and feel what no worldly intelligence may gain.

Look how a simple old poor woman in prayer finds favor through her innocence and sorrow. Who do you think taught her how to pray? No one from this world, but rather grace from above. See too, how a poor innocent uneducated man who lives by his toil, may gain this wisdom perfectly, if he travels to the far country within him, becoming the wisest in the land. Truly he may well be called a Master who points to the name above all names, that he who was without knowledge offers the path to wisdom, that we may reach heights beyond all knowing. We must do what is to be done, and bow the ear of our heart to listen to this learning.

Wisdom is the only gift that God keeps to give sparingly to those whom he will. God has given the office of christening children and the power to baptize and to forgive sins to many, but this gift he safeguards. St John says, 'Here is he who baptizes and forgives sin.' But he grants wisdom sparingly, the wisdom to feel and taste how sweet his providence. Many are gifted with the grace of his Word; but this grace is given to but a few. This precious gift God gives to whom he will and when he will.

The Third and Fourth Rungs: Prayer and Contemplation

We come to realize that we will never achieve through our own power the knowing and feeling of this wisdom. The harder we attempt to climb, the more we come to see that through our own strength and intelligence we are too weak to continue. It is then, finally, that each of us begins to know in our heart how helpless we are. Only then we are at last humbled, falling down with a meek and lowly heart to pray:

'Lord, you will not be seen except to those who are pure of heart. I have done all that is in me, read and thought deeply and searched what it is and in what manner I might best come to this purity that I might somewhat know you. Lord, I have sought and thought with all my poor heart; and, Lord, in my reflections and meditations the fire of desire kindles to know you, not only on the outside, but feeling and tasting your goodness in my soul. Lord, I do not ask for my own benefit, for I am not worthy to enter your house. But as much, Lord, as the dog eats of the crumbs that fall from the table of the lord, I ask of my heritage that is to come one drop of the heavenly joy to comfort my thirsty soul that burns in love longing for you'.

My heart is enflamed with desire and longing. I call out to my Lord as the dear spouse who comes quickly to my mourning soul that languishes in love. What does God whose help is ever poured out upon the righteous by giving ear to our prayer do? He doesn't wait until the prayer is fully ended, but he pierces in the midst of the burning desire of that thirsty soul, and with a secret balm of heavenly sweetness softens the soul and comforts it, and makes it be so overcome with delight and joy that it forgets all earthly things for that hour, and he makes it to lose itself in wonder. In mortal works we are so preoccupied that we lose the guidance of reason and our mind become obsessed with worldly affairs. But throwing off ballast as we climb the ladder of contemplation our fleshly stirrings are quieted. In this moment, in this place, the flesh cannot dominate the spirit.

But, Lord, by what sign may we know when you do this, and what is the token of your coming? Are sighs and tears the messenger of this joy and comfort? And if it be so, it seems marvelous, it seems uncommon that comfort comes with sighs and joy with tears. And it seems they should not be called tears, but heavenly dew that comes from above, that moistens the cheeks, and cleanses the soul within, as a symbol of our baptism. The outer tears are but a sign of the inner. They are innocent tears, through which the inner spots, the stain of sin, are washed away. Blessed are those who weep, for Christ says of them they shall laugh. In these tears the soul recognizes God as true spouse. This is the solace your loving spouse gives you, sighs mingled with tears. But, dear worthy Lord, since these sighs and these tears are so sweet, what great joy and comfort lies ahead for the lovers you have chosen when they first know you and see you as you are. But how can we speak to others of a treasure so hidden and so unknown that they may understand, since none can understand unless they, too, have tasted of that nectar. This is the cry of those whom God has sent such a joy, to share a taste of that sweetness that remains without end. For all that people read in books is nonsense, unless the heart understands.

The Grace of His Presence Comes and Goes for Our Good

My soul, we have talked of this at length. It seems good for us to be here with Peter and John, to have pleasure and joy with our Spouse, and make our dwelling here with him. There is no need to make three booths[iv], for one is enough to shelter us all, that we may be together and have our talking in measurable humor. But what does our Lord say? 'I must go,' he says, 'for the light of the morning is here'. The light and the comfort that you desire, you have. After the blessing is given, and the feast has been consumed, and the namesake of Jacob returned to Israel, then the spouse glides away, taking with him all but the memory of the sweetness sent to his lover in contemplation. Yet the Bridegroom is always present in spirit, through grace and emptying of will.

Be assured that he is always with you, though he is gone for a little while. The paradox is that he must depart to keep you, for your own good. This coming and this going is truly for your benefit, and know well that through this your gains will be great. He comes to you, and he leaves you. He comes to comfort you, and then he leaves you. Be consoled that he comforts you for your holy living. Therefore think well of yourself and leap with Joy. For this reason, our spouse comes and he goes, he brings comfort and he withdraws it leaving us in our weakness to reckon with who we are; yet he lets us somewhat feel how sweet a joy he brings, but before we may fully know him he departs yet again to the far country.

The Three Graces from God

I do not understand my own behavior; I do not act as I mean to, but I do things that I hate, for though the will to do what is good is in me, the power to do it is not. The good thing I want to do, I never do; the evil thing which I do not want – that is what I do'(Romans 7:15-19)

Grace is a gift from the Holy Spirit that insists on our cooperation, for as Paul says, *'we cooperate with God's grace for our own good'* (Phil. 2:13) We open our hearts when he sends us goodness through his grace, and do what we must to keep and to hold it. But we can do nothing to repay, except invite him into our heart. For this reason, it is important to speak of God's grace.

First, Habitual Grace: The first is habitual grace, poured forth by God to all creatures. This is God's help that he, through his goodness, gives to all creatures that they may 'live and move and have their being' (Acts 17:28), and without his grace they can do nothing. As St. Augustine notes, for as all creatures have their being, yet are made from nothing, they are sustained and preserved by his grace, or they will just as surely become dust again. (see St Augustine's 'Enchidrion'), St Paul understood that well when he said, *'That I am, that I am alive, that I see, feel, or go, or stand, all is from God's grace'.*(2 Cor 12:9)

Second, Actual Grace: The second is Actual Grace. This grace God gives us, and is actualized within us, but only if we cooperate and accept it with our free will. This grace stands always at the door of our heart, and knocks upon our free will to ask to enter, as it says in the Luke's Gospel: 'Lo, I stand at the door and knock. Whoever hears my voice and opens the door to me, I shall enter. (Luke 11:0) Here the Lord gently and humbly offers us his merciful grace. This grace is freely given by God. We need to accept this grace when God sends it, and make ourselves ready to be helped by this second grace, that we may be worthy to receive the gift of the Holy Spirit, that moves us to good and guides us away from evil.

For the health of our souls two things are necessary: the first is grace, and the other is free will. Without these two no human can achieve the spiritual health that was lost through the sin of Adam, but instead remains hidden within us. Nothing holy comes of free will without grace, nor grace without our consent. This St Augustine notes when he says, 'Though He created you without your cooperation He does not justify you without your fiat and desire for it." (Writings of St Augustine, Sermon 11, 13)

Our free will cannot of its own power create grace, we may however use God's gift within us to cast out the old self that keeps us from grace, which St Augustine calls cupidity^v which is our selfish nature. Lectio Divina makes us ready to actualize this grace. In other words, you cannot through your own strength give light to the house, but you can turn on a lamp to lighten the house. Who is to blame for your lack of sight if you close your eyes against the light? Similarly, if you will not open your mouth to take food, only you are to blame for going hungry. God says to you, open your mouth. I will fill it with good food. Open your heart to me, and I will fill it with my grace. St Augustine said, 'We do not lack grace because God has not given it'.

The grace of God is ever available to dwell in us. 'God through his omnipotence, so free and so generous, fills all souls according to their readiness to receive.'[vi] We who are moved and called to this grace freely open the gates of our heart, and with our free will grant entry. Once the Holy Spirit dwells in our heart, our labor of love binds us to him as his true companion. Therefore, as the apostle says, 'The grace of God was not missing in me'. (2 Cor 12:9) Rather he showed in his incarnate works that the grace of God poured forth from him. Jesus Christ does so completely for all who make a dwelling place for him. He will not sit idle, for he must do the work of his Father who sent him. Of this grace St Augustine spoke and said, 'This grace is ever available to me, but only if it finds me ready. Wherever I go, he never leaves me.'[ii]

God is our partner and is always ready to work with us. He gives his grace and we reap the bounty promised to us when we give him our works.

Because of our sinful nature we are fooled into believing we can gain every worldly good if we but reach out and snatch it. But instead we lose a piece of our soul every time we inflict injury on others. We give our love to the devil and lust only for the world, withdrawing our love from our gracious Father. As John says in his Epistle, 'Do not love the things of this world'. (1 John 2:15) The charity of the Father sits dormant within the one who loves the world, for all that is in the world desires the flesh, and lusts for mortal life, which is not of the Father, but of the world. But the world shall pass away, and all that is lusted after with it. These things we lust for, contrary to the counsels of our Lord God. We turn our back on that which Our Lord purchased at such a great price with the blood of the undefiled Lamb, Christ Jesus. We separate ourselves from the bliss of our Lord willingly. God says to his people through Isaiah the Prophet, 'My love I shall give to all who are my true servants'. (Isaiah 42:8) Be a true partner to God and he will give you more than your share.

Third Grace: Grace in Action The third grace is known as Caritas: Where Charity and Love Prevail.[vii] This grace is given to those who open their heart and make ready their free will to receive it.

This grace is the gift of the Holy Spirit that moves us to do good deeds. Through our action He seeks our cooperation in pouring his love out to the world, for God is love, and all who live in love, live in God. (1 John 4) Without this grace we are without purpose. This grace rises from the foundation of habitual grace, ever gratuitously present, to actual grace, which is our fiat, our Grace in Action, God pours out his extravagant love to the world through our heart, the manifestation of God's special love.

This grace makes us patient and meek, enduring the loss of worldly goods, loss of worldly friends, bodily harm, and sicknesses. Through this we offer goodness, avoid evil and know all that is good. God offers this gift in earnest so that we might enjoy endless bliss. By this grace the angels speak, 'Hold what you have'. (Rev. 3:11) Hold fast to the grace that God has sent to you, for this grace leads to bliss.

The Parable of the Innkeeper

For those with a deep love of contemplation, God is like the Innkeeper who draws wine connoisseurs to taste his very fine wine, in the hope that they might drink and spend all their money. He knows well when he sees his oenophiles[viii] on the byways. Quietly he goes to them, enticing them as he catches their imagination, tempting them with his excellent claret, in color, swirl, smell, taste, and savor. He draws them to his inn, offering them samples to taste. Soon they thirst for more, because the pleasure from a mere taste is fleeting. Too soon they spend what they have, and then they sell or pawn their coat, their hood and anything the broker will trade, just to try to quench the unquenchable by the promise of that fine vintage.

This is how it is with those who have been richly illuminated by God in contemplation, having tasted His heavenly potion. It is so alluring in richness one can't help but spend the day drinking of the sweetness of God. Then too quickly the bridegroom departs, moving darkened hearts to fasting, giving alms, and doing all sorts of penance. Depleted and spiritually drained, with no more to spend, their earthly possessions are pledged. This was the destiny of apostles, martyrs, and young virgins in their time. Some gave their bodies to burn in fire, some let their heads be cut off, some gave their breasts to be carved from their bodies, and some their bodies to be dragged by wild horses. Yet all their sacrifice, compared to the desire for lasting joy was a small price to pay. But dipping our finger for a taste of the potion of heavenly sweetness, we experience a sampling of the true joy of His presence. All who desire fully to have that perfection need to follow in the footsteps of Christ, continually stirring the flame in their hearts with his love, as these wine connoisseurs did at the Inn.

When God sends any diminished likeness to your soul, know that God speaks to you, and whispers in your ear, and says: 'Take this little portion, taste and see how sweet I am. But if you desire to fully know what you have tasted, run after me and follow the savor of my banquet. Lift up your heart to me where I am sitting on the right hand of my Father, and there you shall see me, not as in a mirror, but face to face. Then you shall have that joy that you have tasted not a passing joy, but forever without end. And that exquisite joy no one can snatch or take from you.

Give God Our Whole Love

Whoever tastes God's sweetness in contemplation and climbs the ladder that stands high, is like Jacob. We must do all in our power to trample under foot all personal worldly wealth, treading under foot indiscretion and sins. The more we cast our worldly cares underfoot, the higher we climb. Then that soul shall be called 'Israel', which means 'One who sees God'; through which sight the soul is fulfilled of that vision that surpasses all others without comparison. Jacob speaks of this struggle in the Book of Genesis: *When the angel realized that Jacob was his match, he said to Jacob, 'Your name will no longer be Jacob, but Israel, because you have struggled with God and with humans and have overcome.'* (Genesis 32;24-32) Jacob is the man who is lifted on high in contemplation. He struggles and strives to know God with all his might. But then at last he overcomes the angel. Likewise, the soul comes to know God through contemplation, for the deepest yearnings of the soul are quenched with such sweetness. One sees that the wealth of the world is useless, for worldly love never quenches and desires of the world dry up. The love of God is whole and sound, and made ever stronger. When God stands unshakable as he steadies the ladder, no suffering of this world can overcome us. As God supports the four rungs of the ladder, we grow in the wisdom of Holy Scripture as pure love.

As God's lover, be watchful and wary, and understand the ways he, your beloved spouse, seems to withdraw from you. Know well that he never withdraws from you, though it may seem that way. He sees you and is all around you. He is watchful day and night. Be prepared, for at an hour you do not expect, the Bridegroom will return. Who, then, is the faithful and prudent bride, whom the master has put his trust in? 'Blessed is that servant whom his master on his arrival finds doing so'. (Matthew 24:44-46) God will have no lover in between. He will have all or leave all. He will have all your love, if in bliss you will be his companion. He is most noble and fair. He demands nothing but what is honest and fair. If you desire to be with him, you must strive for a chaste and holy life.

Beware Of Unfaithfulness

Be ever mindful of worldly things once you return to your daily cares from contemplation. Since the reflections and ponderings of the heart make us fragile in our new-found innocence, as happens in contemplation, we may feel the weakness of the flesh, like a yoke around our neck that draws us downwards into a spiritual dark night, blocking us from the brightness of the true light. Since we must descend down the same stairs we had just climbed, it is good that we come down in degrees, warily and gently so that we not hurt ourselves. Take rest now and then and let our free will be restored gently, taking whatever time you need to return with the shield to your heart securely in place.

There are four possible causes that imperil us. The first are physiological needs that cannot be prevented. The second, fear for our mortal safety. This third is false insecurity that we are not loved and do not belong. And the fourth is sinful pride. The first does not harm, the second may be permitted, the third is distressing, but the fourth requires reconciliation and penance. It's hard to believe that once we've climbed the highest rung of the ladder, having tasted that heavenly sweetness, the possibility that from such height we can fall and be trapped by worldly desires. But we can be tricked into thinking we can bite of the forbidden fruit, believing we will taste honey, only to find bitter gall. Here we enter a period of grief and sorrow. In despair we falsely believe that it would be better to not have known God at all rather than to have known and have to leave and go back.

How can you return to God with such sin? God might well say, 'From nothing I made you, perfect and righteous, only to have you sin, enslaving yourselves. Then I sent my only Son to die a terribly unjust death. Indeed, with the ultimate price I paid the ransom. I bought you from slavery. Then again and again you ignored my commandments and dared to run with the sinful of this world. But every time, I lifted you from them, and before others gave you my grace, for I wanted you close to me. And when I would have made my dwelling with you, you shut me out as a stranger. When my prophets spoke my words to you, you cast them behind you, and followed the vanities of the world and the desires of the flesh.'

After fully examining our conscience we must pledge and offer penance. Kneel before the steps of his holy altar, crying out: "Dear, worthy Lord, sweet friend, wise counselor, and so strong a helper, I was foolish and unwise to cast you aside, you who are so gentle of heart." Ah, how we lament, knowing firsthand the shame of Adam and Eve! How tragic a change this is, to turn away from our Maker, our Lover, but all is now dark and lost, our hearts and lives so empty without Him.

Having once felt that secret abiding of the Holy Spirit filling our soul, we cast ourselves down with wicked thoughts and vanity. It is not right that ears that had just heard His Eternal Word should instead stoop to vain tales and backbiting; and the eyes, that just now were baptized with holy tears, should turn its gaze to vanities; and the tongue that had just offered tokens of love and petitions with love and praise after being drawn with cords of love, should now have such joy turn to a world full of vanity, foul speech, cursing and swearing.

But Jesus Christ in his compassion lifts us yet again, if we but return to him, our true Physician who heals the sick, our Shepherd who comforts the contrite of heart.

To him we joyfully pray:

Help us, Lord, to remove all obstacles that hinder us from loving you. Lift us up the ladder until we see your face shine upon us, where we might enjoy the sweetness of divine contemplation; not drop by drop, nor now and then, but where they are ever fulfilled with the torrent of pleasure and have that joy that no worldly temptation can take away. Heavenly Father, preserve us unstained in peace unchangeable. Amen!

Guigo the Carthusian

Part II
The Spanish Mystics

Spanish Mystics: Three Great Saints from the Spanish Peninsula

Beginning with my early adult life the study of the lives and writings of mystics has been a focused interest for me. After reading some of the quotes from the sixteenth century writings of St. Teresa of Avila on Christian spirituality I added her books to my library: the Way of Perfection, the Interior Castle, the Letters of St Teresa, and Flames of Love (collected poems of St Teresa and St John of the Cross).

Later when I became familiar with St. John of the Cross and his works from the same period, I augmented my library with his Dark Night of the Soul, Ascent of Mount Carmel, the Spiritual Canticle, and the Living Flame of Love.

Some years later I came upon the biography of St Ignatius of Loyola. I was fascinated with his intellect, logical mind, military training and the circumstances leading up to the injury to his leg that abruptly ended his career as a soldier. Providentially, during his convalescence he developed his groundbreaking logical thesis about the movements of the spirit as he assessed his own experiences of desolations and consolations. This work became the foundation of Ignatian Spirituality and led him to become the great saint he is.

Interested as I am with the historical context of the lives of the saints, I noticed the intersections of these three lifelines. Their stories became the sparks that fanned the active imagination of my young mind. Remarkably we have three great names of Catholic mysticism born on the Spanish peninsula within a 50 year time period.

As with the stories of all the saints, none of these three set out to take up the cause of defending the Church. It was St Ignatius and the Society of Jesus, by his disposition, that naturally came to defend the challenges of Protestantism. The collected works of these three contributed to the great achievements of the Catholic Reformation. Their writings became the hallmark of what is known as Reformation Mystical Spirituality.

Both St. Teresa and St. John were called to the Religious life. They took the permanent vows of the Order of Carmelites. After meeting each other, they were convinced that their cause was to reform the Order of Carmelites in radical ways that would place both of them in harm's way. This was particularly true for St. John, whose brothers of his own Order resorted to violence to keep him from upsetting their comfortable lives. They captured him and hid him away in a dank dungeon cell. During St John's time of incarceration he suffered greatly. In fact, the torture he endured nearly took his life. Through his suffering he gave himself completely to God, and was rewarded with enlightenment that inspired him to compose his famous "Dark Night of the Soul."

In that work, he uses the metaphor of the dark night in two significant ways. He ponders the inability of the intellect to grasp God, and then describes the experience of the soul on its journey to the mountaintop, to mystical union. The dark night of the senses and the dark night of the spirit describe movements of purification and intensified prayer which lead to a deepening relationship with God. In St. John's thinking, the closer we get to God the more it appears as though nothing is happening -- God's presence is absent and life is less attractive. Of his concept of the "senses," St. John discovered something profound which has become widely accepted -- the inadequacy of any concept or image to describe God. He was to give classic expression to the experience of being spiritually lost, confused, feeling panic, and increasingly feeling trapped in a spiritual drought. His journaling of the dark night is a blessing for many. This includes myself, as it is a part of my own spiritual journey. I've come to know this "dark night" as the Pilgrim's Way of the Cross.

Carmelite Perspective

For Carmelites Lectio Divina is an authentic source of Christian Spirituality which they practice every day. Through this practice they develop a deep and genuine love for Lectio Divina. This is their primary method to foster growth in the surpassing knowledge of Christ. In this way they live the Apostle Paul's commandment, a crucial part of their Rule[ix]:

"Let the sword of the spirit, the Word of God, live abundantly in your mouth and in your hearts; and whatever you must do, do it in the name of the Lord."

Carmelite spiritual exercises are similar to Guigo's four movements. The goal of every Carmelite is to give one hundred percent of themselves to God, leaving everything of this world behind.

Lectio Divina

Lectio: Careful repetitious recitation

Meditatio: An effort to fathom the meaning

Oratio: A personal response to God

Contemplatio: Experiential contact with the divine

Lectio – Reading
Reading is the careful repetitious recitation of a short passage of Scripture.

Meditatio – Meditation
Meditation is an effort to fathom the meaning of the text and make it personally relevant to oneself in Christ

Oratio – Prayer
Prayer in the context of a personal response to the relevant Scriptural passage, petitioning God for the divine grace of the text as it applies to the individual and their personal prayer intentions, in order to move toward a closer union with God.

Contemplatio -- Contemplation
To contemplate is to gaze at length on something. The idea behind this final element is that sometimes, by the infused grace of God, one is raised above meditation to a state of seeing or experiencing the text as mystery and reality; one comes into experiential contact with the One behind and beyond the text. It is an exposure to the divine presence, to God's truth and benevolence.

Within the construct of Carmelite Spirituality, meditation and contemplation are two entirely distinct and separate movements. For Carmelites, meditation can be initiated by the person. Contemplation, on the other hand, is a supernatural state of awareness in which the soul is raised by God, if only for a brief moment, to a state of being and reality that is higher and closer to God than the person is capable of achieving solely on one's own efforts. Unlike the first three movements, contemplation is a pure gift from God. Keeping this in mind might well prevent unnecessary frustration and anxiety. Contemplation is a passive state for the disciple. God will raise you up and carry you into his Sacred Heart, but of *his* initiation, not yours.

St. John of the Cross

Lectio Divina played an important role in the contemplative prayer life of St. John of the Cross. For him Holy Scripture was the first of the four "sources" of Christian life and spirituality, along with the Church and its ministers, experience and science. Scripture was fundamental in his life and essential in his personal relationship with God. We see this throughout his writings on his vision of Lectio Divina.

St John came to the realization that the nature of absolute love was mystical union, that experience of direct communion between the soul and God. The soul lives united in that which it loves.[x]

Prayer for St John leads to unbound gratitude and longing. The more we are blessed to experience what God gives us, the greater our desire to be emptied so that we might be filled with goodness and holiness. As divine flow pours from us in answer to prayer, we have need of nothing, taking on the liberation of poverty.

His prayer ultimately led St. John to go beyond anything that can be known. In his writings he speaks of a journey into an unknown land, experiencing illumination, yet returning to unknowing.

Wisdom in unknowing, for St John, overwhelms and transcends all knowledge. Some years ago I was absorbed in his writings. Taking on, bit by bit, a clarity of his teachings on the dark night. As it happened, I met a Spanish graduate student at University of Michigan in Ann Arbor who was quite excellent at translating ancient Basque writings. I introduced him to a facsimile of St John's poem, "Telling the Transfiguration," penned in ancient Basque. Over the next several weeks, he and I worked to translate the work into this text:

Telling the Transfiguration

I entered into the unknown
Yet when I saw myself there
Without knowing where I was
I understood great things;
I cannot say what I felt
For I remained in unknowing
Transcending all knowledge.

That perfect wisdom
Was of peace and holiness
Held in profound solitude;
It was something so secret
That I was left stammering,
Transcending all knowledge.

I was so overwhelmed,
So absorbed and withdrawn,
That my senses were left
Hollowed of their sensing,
And my spirit was given
An understanding
while not understanding,
Transcending all knowledge.

One who truly arrives there
Cuts free from oneself;
All that was known before
Now seems worthless,
And wisdom so soars
That one is left in unknowing
Transcending all knowledge.

The higher you ascend
The less you will understand,
Because the cloud is dark
Which lit up the night;
Whoever knows this
Remains always in unknowing
Transcending all knowledge.

This wisdom in unknowing
Is so overwhelming
That intellectual debate
Can never conquer it,
For knowledge cannot reach
To the understanding of not-understanding,
Transcending all knowledge.

And this supreme wisdom
Is so exalted
That no power of man or learning
Can grasp it;
He who empties himself
Will, with wisdom in unknowing,
Always be transcending.

And if you should want to hear:

The highest wisdom lies
In the loftiest sense
Of the essence of God;
This is a work of His mercy,
To leave one without knowing,
Transcending all knowledge.[xi]

Saint John of the Cross (24-June-1542 – 14 Dec 1591), born Juan de Yepes Alvarez.

His studies and poetry on the maturity of the soul is the summit of mystical Spanish literature. St. John of the Cross was canonized a saint in 1726 by Pope Benedict XIII. He is one of the thirty-three Doctors of the Church. In 1969 his feast day was moved to his date of death, December 14th. Job's thoughts tie beautifully to St John's:

He reveals the deep things of darkness
and brings deep shadows into the light. (Job 12:22)

Our soul moves to darkness even as we yearn to journey toward the light of Christ. In darkness, the journey has barely begun. For St. John wisdom was not something learned or acquired. It is given to us by God. A gift revealed in the dark night of the soul.

The Master Beggar in the Carmelite Tradition

There is another ancient practice rooted in Carmelite Spirituality, of which I have spent many hours in prayer. Carmelites have desired to be so emptied of all desire except the burning urgings of the Sacred Heart of Jesus, that hours and hours are spent in Lectio Divina, seeking to be a novice of the Master Beggar. The Master Beggar is Jesus of Nazareth, poor, and humble, begging on the street corner. The goal of the novice is to pass the ultimate test. To be so free of any mortal pleasures and treasures and attachments that Jesus trusts them to stand in for him. This poem arose from just such an illuminating moment for me.

Worse off than the poorest man
alive, stood the street corner beggar,
Blind eyes staring with
steaming breath,
Shaming those who pass.
That is what you are to me,
Jesus of Nazareth.

Must you take up your post on
this block on this particular day?
Do I have nowhere to hide from
you?
Is there no corner of the earth
where I can find sanctuary
from your sad face,
Your whispered plea?

I seek the glass-topped counters
of the merchant's gleaming shops,
But make no purchases for You
are there, blind eyes unseeing,
A reflection in the shining
storefront window.
How can I waste one coin while
you implore,
With tear-soiled cheeks and
dark dirt-matted hair?

And when I extend to You as
charity a few pennies offered in love,
You stand ever still, fixing your
sorrowful wide-eyed gaze on me.
Must I surrender every last cent
of my possessions
to your outreached hand?

Jesus, my street corner beggar,
how much would you take from me?
My father and mother? The
spouse I long to know?
The child I cherish tenderly?
Even the blood that through my
heart and hands flow?

I too should be a beggar.
Long tormented, my dream is to
surrender all and stand for You
On some bleak wind-swept
inner city corner,
Tear-streaked and dirt-
matted...
And trouble humankind to
search within,
To depths of compassion for its
human heart.

Ignatian Perspective

At the heart of St Ignatius' spirituality is Ignatius' imaginative and sensorial approach to meditating on Gospel passages. This approach brought healing and dramatic life change to him.

Ignatius the Spaniard was a soldier in battle with the French and his leg was hit by a cannonball. When he was convalescing in bed for months of recovery he wanted to read popular fantasy novels about romance and chivalry that he enjoyed, but none were available. Instead he was given a book on the life of Christ that featured Gospel stories. Meditating on these with his imagination brought him great comfort — and salvation from sin and healing of his body. He went on to found the Society of Jesus and teach his approach to discernment while seeking an encounter with Christ by visualizing ourselves in the Gospel stories.

When an individual made a retreat in the pattern of his Spiritual Exercises he invited the Retreatant to pray to come to know Christ so that one may love him in a more real way and following from this knowledge and love become a more faithful disciple.

In order to grow in this faith knowledge, Ignatius invited the Retreatant to engage in a prayer method called *imaginative contemplation*. In contrast with the Carmelite tradition, his is not a form of mystical prayer, but rather a method that employees the use of the three plains of the senses (see lesson 1). In an imaginative way this method leads you to reflect on a Gospel passage, seeing, hearing, tasting, touching, and smelling the Gospel scene as it is brought real and alive. Using the imagination, you immerse yourself in it imaginatively. You feel the heat of the day, smell the livestock and clouds of dust on the road, listen to Jesus' words, and watch his actions. It's a way to engage the gospel personally, utilizing all of our faculties.

Through this time-tested technique we have yet another method for praying with the heart of the Church.

The Ignatian Movements of Lectio Divina[xii]

Lectio Divina

Lectio: Careful repetitious recitation

Meditatio/Contemplatio: An effort to fathom the meaning

Oratio: Heartfelt Prayer

Lectio: Reading Scripture

Select a passage from one of the Gospels in which Jesus is interacting with others. Recall what one is doing in engaging with the Word of God and what one desires from this encounter. God is present and because God is present one relies on God. St. Ignatius suggested reading the Gospel passage twice so that the story and the details of the story become familiar.

Meditatio/Contemplatio: Meditation and Imaginative Contemplation:

Close your eyes and reconstruct the scene in your imagination. Place yourself in the time and place and watch the men and women in the scene. What does Jesus look like? How do the others react to him? What are the people saying to one another? What emotions fill their words? Is Jesus touching someone? As you enters into the scene, desire to be there. Place yourself in the scene, perhaps as an observer, as crying out to Jesus for healing, or as one helping others approach Jesus.

Some people's imaginations are very active so they construct a movie-like scenario with a Gospel passage. Others will enter the scene with verbal imagination, reflecting on the scene and mulling over the actions. Vividness is not a criteria to be effective at this point. Engagement is, and the result is a more interior knowledge of Jesus.

Oratio: Heartfelt Prayer

As you finishes, take time for prayer. Take a moment to speak person to person with Christ saying what comes from the heart.

Further Study

Scripture Passages for Ignatius' Spiritual Exercises are available to download at no cost. Available are the "Lectio Divina Guides" and "Experiences", Ignatian Meditation Guides that are ready made personal prayer or small groups. These downloadable Gospel passages are the same ones recommended by Ignatius in The Spiritual Exercises in his chapter on "The Mysteries of the Life of Christ Our Lord." They are kept in his order, grouped according to the four week themes in his program, and follow his distinctive methodology for Scripture meditation.

For more information navigate your web browser to:
http://www.soulshepherding.org

My Ignatian 8 Day Retreat Journal

As part of my priestly formation I attended an 8 day Ignatian retreat. Prior to this retreat, I had attended quite a few seminars on Ignatian Spirituality, weekend retreats, and, later, a 30 day retreat. For my 8 day retreat I had a pretty good working knowledge of the Discernment of Spirits, Ignatian Lectio Divina, and the Ignatian Examen. I attended this retreat in the early summer at Creighton University in Omaha. It was a perfect setting for my experience.

Important to the spiritual journey is journaling. I kept it all, included in what I call my Faith365 journal. This journal is circular, and comes around every year on my calendar. Year by year the journal builds. This gives me a retrospective of my spiritual journey over the years. To give you a deeper sense of Ignatian Lectio Divina, I have included excerpts of my journal for the 8 day journey. The format for the daily journal:

- Daily Intention
- Scripture passage
- The Retreatant's reflection
- The Retreatant's prayer

Day One

Intention: To be able to be generous and to receive a new inner taste of Your love for me, Lord.

> For Zion's sake I will not keep silent,
> for Jerusalem's sake I will not remain quiet,
> till her righteousness shines out like the dawn,
> her salvation like a blazing torch.
>
> The nations will see your righteousness,
> and all kings your glory;
> you will be called by a new name
> that the mouth of the LORD will bestow. Isaiah 62

"Live in accord with the spirit and you will not yield to the cravings of the flesh. The fruit of the spirit is love, joy, peace, patient endurance, kindness, generosity, faith mildness and chastity. Let us follow the spirit's lead." Gal 5:16-25

I opened my window and listed to the cars on route 80. I watch the lights stream, bright headlights coming toward me, red taillights moving away. I imagine every third car to be a Catholic family, and wonder how I might invest myself with the Holy Spirit to bring them closer to Christ. I wonder if the desolation and spiritual darkness I I struggled with this past winter was a collective manifestation of the loss of hope felt by the those sitting in these cars, and I pray for them. In my imagination, I adopt them as my freeway congregation.

St Philip Neri said, *"He who wants something other than Christ, does not know what he wants. He who seeks something other than Christ, does not know what he wishes. He who works and not for Christ does not know what he is doing."* Like Isaiah, St Neri put his trust in the positive, in grace. He trusted in the love of God, which would do its work in men of itself like a fire, or a seed – unnoticed and hidden at first, but already growing.

Isaiah gives me hope.

I understood what my Spiritual Director saw as he look up at the assembly in the auditorium last night: 177 men on fire with the Lord, men that are yet unnoticed like a hidden seed, but already growing. They will soon bring the Word Incarnate to thousands of souls. They will give hope where the wick is smoldering. People across the land will soon be reminded that they were all conceived with the Lord's Purpose.

My Freeway Congregation moves to and fro, up and down the highway. Will they be blinded by what has become the distracting secular culture, or will they perhaps look beyond, to the Star of Hope rising on the distant horizon.

Day Two

Intention: That God draw us with human cords, with bands of love.

When Israel was a child I loved him, out of Egypt I called my son.

The more I called them, the farther they went from me, Sacrificing to the Baals and burning incense to idols.

Yet it was I who taught Ephraim to walk, who took them in my arms; I drew them with human cords, with bands of love; I fostered them like one who raises an infant to his cheeks; Yet, though I stooped to feed my child, they did not know that I was their healer. Hosea 11: 1-4

In this reading from Hosea, we are called to change allegiances from the sin that is lord of our lives to the Lord who can "take away the sin of the world." When we let go of our secret attachment to sin, our true identity emerges. We are children of God, but the only path to this realization is through unrelenting mercy. A loving Father who raises an infant to his cheeks is the true agent of mercy. Through Sacred Scripture we gain the wisdom to realize that what comes easy to us is to judge and destroy life and what comes hard to us is to be open to steadfast love and forgiveness. In the penitential rite of the Mass, the Kyrie Eleison, we say three times that the knot has been cut and we are free. This mercy exercise unties this knot we have tied to our worst moments.

My prayer today is to rediscover my True Self. Dear Lord, bring to the light of day those dark corners of my soul where I desire to be "as gods" – those places where I seek omnipotence, the power to have everything I want; to have all my wishes and desires satisfied. This day, lead me to conversion. Shift my center from fear and pride to the self-giving love and service to God and others. Lord, help me rediscover my True Self. My Imago Dei, the Image of God within who is Love.

Our cultural belief systems are changing. "Faith" becomes faith in a human-made system. We are encouraged to have "faith" that our government will take make sure everything is fine. The "Greatest

Good" we can understand is the societal good. For a species with unlimited imagination we sure can limit ourselves. The dominant emphasis of society is very much focused on anything but a spiritually based "First Principal" of our God-given Purpose – our incarnational intentional life. The highest "First Principal" can only be as high as one's perceived Ideal. And if one's isn't mystical union then we're not aiming high enough.

We are instead trained to be happy and content with the secondary principals of leading lawful and productive lives. These usurp and become our "First Principals." Something has been lost, and that "something" is something unreachable for a people living in a space where one's "First Principal" is based on a materially based faith. The "something" that needs to be rediscovered is instead hidden in wonder and awe. When we enter into child-like mystery and wonder and awe we are raised to God-given wisdom that can only be gained through Grace -- wisdom that leads us to Christ.

Wisdom leads us to a place where Christ is present in the Eucharist
Because "Nothing IS impossible with God."

Wisdom leads us to a place where Christ is present in the Word.
Because "Nothing IS impossible with God."

Wisdom leads us to a place where Christ is present in each other"
Because "Nothing IS impossible with God."

How do I obtain clean hands and a pure heart? How do I seek to desire not worthless things? In my busyness much is demanded of me. How do I come to be led to restful streams. I long for the music of the angel's 10-stringed lyre. Give me the grace to sit a spell in your presence. Envelop me in your mystery. Let me be emptied of my restlessness. Gently raise me to your cheek. Show me your ways. Give me the wisdom to understand that with you nothing is impossible. Teach me to be your instrument.

He chose us in him before the creation of the world
to be holy and blameless in his sight. Ephesians 1:3-4

I frequently think about my relationship with my son, Sean. Before he was knitted in his mother's womb, I knew him. In my late teens, and into my twenties I would sit and imagine him. If I ever had a son, his name would be "Sean." I have tasted the love of Abba to His children. We are loved for eternity, and we are knitted in a particular fashion at the moment of our conception.

I have been a spiritual director to some that had no security as a child. It can take years of seeking and understanding the love of Abba to heal the deep wounds of a distressed childhood.

I pray that the Holy Spirit imbue my heart with the grace of God, turn away from sin and be filled with love. May our families be holy families so that we might teach the world around us the treasure of perfect love. May we feel God's love in our hearts. May we come to know his choice that made us in his likeness, each Children of the Father.

Day Three

Intention: To be able to taste interior amazement in the face of your magnanimous goodness and the beauty of your love for me, as your creature, Lord.

> *"For where your treasure is, there also will your heart be."*
> *Luke 12:22-32*

I wonder about us being capable of deification. How does that work? Isn't that the sin of pride of Adam and Eve? Their sin killed them. Yet we hear we can be adopted Sons of Daughters of God, thanks be to Christ who died on the cross to be our redeemer. Jesus, the New Adam reversed the sin of the first Adam. So tell me again how we are capable of being deified, without recommitting Adams sin? For much of my life I seek to be ruler of my own universe. But the great saints say over and over that through the Incarnate Christ every man has regained the power of deification.

The key to this puzzle perhaps is to watch the Son.

> *"... he emptied himself, taking the form of a slave, coming in*
> *human likeness. He humbled himself, becoming obedient to death,*
> *even death on a cross."Phil 2:2*

In the second chapter of Philippians, Paul goes to tell us to be obedient to the Father. For God is the one, for his good purpose, who works in us to desire the Kingdom of God and to do his holy works.

This Son who is fully God and fully man, was steadfastly obedient to his Father. So much so in fact that he emptied himself. That is part of the key to understand deification: steadfast obedience to the Father. But obedience isn't enough. Jesus taught us that in the Beatitudes,

> *"unless your righteousness surpasses that of the scribes and*
> *Pharisees, you will not enter the Kingdom of Heaven." Matt 5:20*

There is a difference between desiring to be a god and being deified, which is gained through the gift of grace. Christ was perfect love. Grace helps us ascend in our ascetic journey, and Christ, meeting us in the middle, will draw us to himself in mystical union. All of these thoughts arose from the final verse of today's scripture passage.

If our thoughts words and actions resolve to narcissistic motives, then our treasures are perishable and we will die, as did Adam and Eve. But if we, in a self-donating act of kenosis empty ourselves, make our way God's way, we will taste the interior amazement of being in the face of God's extravagant goodness and love for us. Then, our every thought words and action will be right-ordered and salvific.

Last night I was asked by my spiritual director to exercise my faith as a gift to say "thank you for being with me in the pain, in the sorrow, in the joy." After spending a year ministering to the aged and infirm at St Patrick Manor in Framingham, Mass, I can use the saintly example of the many wonderful friends I made, many of whom died over the course of the year. The Carmelite Sisters of the Aged and Infirm, and in particular Sr. Brigid Riley, taught me how to accept the "thank you" from the souls in their care.

What started out as a burden, being confronted with so many in chronic need, turned into a year of grace. Many were bedridden, many were suffering from Alzheimer's, many were grotesquely crippled and deformed, most couldn't walk on their own.

When I visited and sat with the residents, they transformed before my eyes into Children of God – transfigured as Christ was on Mount Tabor. These Children of God had much more to give to me than what I came to offer them.

In retrospect, I started the year being unwittingly "admitted" to St Patrick Manor as the most aged and infirm of the bunch, tricked into thinking that I was there to minister, only to later learn that I was the patient admitted for treatment. I entered spiritually old and crippled. I was discharged full of youthful vigor. They had me drink from the Holy Fountain of Youth. I was caressed tenderly by their holiness, and I learned from them the miracle of gratitude – a gratitude to Jesus their Savior and their closest friend.

Day Four

Intention: To be able to taste and receive a new sense of my frailty and the goodness of depending on Your absolute love for me, Lord.

"We saw his star at its rising and have come to do him homage."
Matthew 2:1-12

The star was a problem. If it hadn't appeared, Jesus would have been much safer. It was the cause of the extreme danger that beset the Holy Family. It led the wise men to Jesus, and it riled the anger of Herod. Babies were slaughtered because of that star.

The star is "a problem" that won't go away. We can't rewrite the Book. No matter how much we wish upon that star, we need to deal with it. Deal with the fact that it was part of God's divine plan.

We all have a built in homing device, planted in our hearts. This homing device, triggered by grace, causes us to be catapulted from our comfort zone. One day we're sitting leisurely on the front porch rocking chair of life, the next we are propelled forward on a life changing pilgrimage -- a new life that is thrilling and yet fraught with peril and danger. Sometimes we go with intentional steps, but often we try to scamper into the night, futilely running to escape God's call, longing to return to that front porch rocking chair. We eventually become so "Son" scorched that we simply have no choice but to abandon ourselves to the outrageous and absolute love of the Lord.

"I know that after my departure savage wolves will come among you."Acts 20:29

I was meditating on the Acts of the Apostles when the sound of a voice rose in my ear. It was the voice of a wise old woman, resplendent in her prose. She recited carefully. Her well-annunciated words still ring in my ear.

The Lord chases us in the wild places of the heart.
Wolves come, and we scatter,
too quick our dark night. No thought or plan
as we hasten...
hasten down the wind.

One minute, the comfort of pasture.
The next -- that terrible flight,
oft times for years...
It all feels so random...
as we hasten,
hasten down the wind.

In the wild places of the heart
we long for a clearing,
an eventual end of night.
The ripening of the fruit of our hastening...
Hastening down the wind.

A mirage ahead? No. Wait!
Safety! The next stop on our pilgrim's journey
A mountain at a breathtaking height.
Our eyes are not fooled by the stinging of sand
Swept up and swirling about
Hastening down the wind.

The Lord chases us in the wild places of the heart.
Hidden a distance from our frightened and blinded sight.
As we hasten,
Hasten down the wind
And into that terrible dark night.

Perhaps it wasn't a wolf (in hindsight)
Perhaps it was a bloodied lamb
In wolf's clothing.
The ripened fruit of the wild places of the heart
Sweeping and swirling
Hastening down the wind.

I long to return to "My front porch rocking chair." Near the end of the book of Jonah, God provided a gourd plant that grew up over Jonah's head, giving shade that relieved him of any discomfort. Jonah was very happy. This was Jonah's "Front porch rocking chair." But God sent a worm to attacked the plant, and it withered. The sun beat down upon Jonah's head till he became faint. Jonah was angry over this. I don't know about you, but I can relate to that. I hated losing my comfortable spot. But God reminds us, *"You are concerned over the plant which cost you no labor and which you did not raise."* I think God was saying, *"What right do you have being angry or sad over losing your Front Porch Rocking Chair."* You ran to the *"Wild Places of the Heart"* to escape my call, but I let no harm come to you.

In the quiet, the Lord speaks to me: "David, I need to send you to places like Nineveh, where 'there are people that cannot distinguish their right hand from their left.' (see Jonah 4:11) My Book lays collecting dust on a forgotten shelf. I gave them a star to guide them, but its brightness blinded them, for they have been in the dark for too long."

"You ran to the 'wild places of the heart.' Your imagination was too restricted to see the new 'Front Porch Rocking Chair' I have in mind for you. Today I give you new sight. Take it. See my goodness. You can depend on me for absolute love."

Holy Spirit, guide me.
Star of David, illuminate me.
Son of Abraham, invite me.
Shepherd of the pasture, watch over me.

Jesus I thank you
for all you've given me
I'm amazed at how you've blessed my life
Jesus I thank you
For the works you've done through me
Amen

Day Five

Intention: To be able to heal from any inner lies or attitudes of heart that prevent me from receiving and staying with Your love for me, Lord.

"Joseph ...take the child and his mother and escape to Egypt. Stay there until I tell you... And so was fulfilled what the Lord had said through the prophet: "Out of Egypt I called my son." Matt 2:13-15

"When Israel was a child, I loved him,
and out of Egypt I called my son.
But the more I called Israel,
the further they went from me." Hosea 11:1

A wise parent knows that children will pull away from their parents at some point as they grow. As a parent, I didn't have this happen until my son's college years. Even though I knew it would happen, it didn't lessen the pain of the "empty nest" syndrome. Even though we are now separated by hundreds of miles my heartstrings are still very much attached. *"I led them with cords of human kindness, with ties of love; I lifted the yoke from their neck and bent down to feed them."* All the wisdom I gained as a parent, God had given me. He experienced all this with his "child" Israel. The more he calls us, the further we go from him – until we gain the wisdom and grace to cast our eyes lovingly back to Abba.

From birth, Jesus suffered greatly with the Holy Family. Herod, representing our evil inclinations, set out to destroy the human icon of All That Is Good. I wonder if it is from this lashing out of evil against every good that we get the expression "All good things must come to an end." Christ taught us otherwise. It may appear to some that evil crushed the good on Good Friday, but Christ is the Victor. He blinded the Evil One to his divinity. All That Is Good triumphed on Golgotha.

From the day of his birth, Jesus was "a sign of contradiction" (Luke 2:34), and he continues to be so, even today. The Lord of hosts, "whose origin is from old, from ancient days" (Mic 5:2), wished to inaugurate his Kingdom by being born Bethlehem. Amid every kind of contradiction, the stones continue to cry out this "good news", the message of redemption which Bethlehem, above all others, is called to proclaim to the world. Here, in a way which surpassed every human hope and expectation, God kept his promises. In the birth of his Son, he revealed the coming of a Kingdom of love: a divine love which stoops down in order to bring healing and lift us up; a love which is revealed in the humiliation and weakness of the Cross, yet triumphs in a glorious resurrection to new life. Christ brought a Kingdom which is not of this world, yet a Kingdom which is capable of changing this world, for it has the power to change hearts, to enlighten minds and to strengthen wills. By taking on our flesh, with all its weaknesses, and transfiguring it by the power of his Spirit, Jesus has called us to be witnesses of his victory over sin and death."

From this painting, "Rest on the Flight to Egypt"[xiii] we see a desolate and lonely landscape, represented with sand that is collected around everything. It reminds us not only of the fulfillment of the prophecy from Hosea, but also the startling and sad truth that Jesus' "desert experiences" did not wait until the time of his public ministry. This was Jesus' first desert experience. He is the source of the only light in the picture. He lies in his mother Mary's bosom, where she lies in the arms of the ancient sphinx. The sphinx is a female monster, a "strangler" that devoured anyone unable to solve her riddle. She asks passersby the most famous riddle in history: "Which creature in the morning goes on four legs, at mid-day on two, and in the evening upon three, and the more legs it has, the weaker it be?" She strangled and devoured anyone unable to answer. Mary, in her Wisdom, answered: "Man—who crawls on all fours as a baby, then walks on two feet as an adult, and then walks with a cane in old age." Ancient Christian tradition tells how this riddle, later taught by Mary to her young Jesus, foreshadowed John 21:

"I tell you the truth, when you were younger you dressed yourself and went where you wanted; but when you are old you will stretch out your hands, and someone else will dress you and lead you where you do not want to go." Jesus said this to indicate the kind of death by which Peter would glorify God. Then he said to him, "Follow me!"

Follow me! Into the desert, says Jesus. I know desert. In meditation he invites me to the terrible vortex of the Christian Lesson.

The "desert experiences" of my life have been challenging yet life changing. In my meditation I consider the role that sand plays in the experience.

Holy Spirit Storm

I see the Holy Family in flight enveloped by a sandstorm. Mary protectively shields and covers her child absolutely and complete, pressing his wrapped body to hers. Joseph and Mary battle the grit that enters ears, nose and mouth. Every step is like a step in quicksand as they push on. Mary takes pity on the donkey, and dismantles. Joseph is pleading but Mary is conscious that the poor animal has taken on their suffering and can bear the heavy burden of the Christ Child no more. The sun sits high, nearly obliterated by the sand, casting the scene into late dusk; a darkened day that foreshadows Christ's Last Earthly Day.

Herod's soldiers, too, have had an exhausting time pursuing the Radiant Child. Usually there is gossip and rumors from the folk that serve as a guidance system for Herod's evil purposes, gossip and rumors that are road signs that lead to their prey. But tonight there is no news. There is only the wind, and an eerie howling silence. The village folk huddle safely behind locked doors. An inner voice warns them to wait out the storm.

In some primitive infant way, Jesus knows this storm is good. He knows it is the work of the Holy Spirit. Joseph has to trust Mary's instinct that this is so. Trust comes hard when you are fighting for your family's life against the double hard luck of Herod and a sandstorm. Yet there is hope for Mary and Joseph, as this New "Son" radiates the scene.

From a Wisdom only God can explain, Jesus knows this storm is good. He knows it is the work of the Holy Spirit. What Jesus knows is passed to Mary. Joseph must trust that this is so. This is a trust not easily come by in such a perilous moment, but he has no other options but than to surrender to faith. Trust comes hard when you are fighting for your family's life against the double hard luck of Herod and a sandstorm. Yet there is hope for Mary and Joseph, as this New "Son" radiates the scene.

Sand of Time

The Holy Family breaks for dry camp at the sphinx. The sand nearly covers everything. It reminds us that all things mortal shall pass, even this great sphinx will someday be buried in time, yet the newly inaugurated Kingdom of God will radiate its message for eternity.

Sand as Symbol of the Mystery

We can feel the effect of wind, but we can't really see it. But we can see the sand as it is blown by the wind. The same with the Holy Spirit. There are symbols all around us if we but open our eyes.

Baby Jesus, illuminate me.
Mother Mary, invite me.
Joseph, her most chaste spouse, watch over me.

Holy Spirit,
guide me through my inner senses to feel attitudes of heart
that prevent me from receiving and staying with the love of my Lord.

Amen!

Day Six

Intention: To be able to receive a new taste of joy in Your healing forgiveness for my sinfulness, Lord.

"Put out into deep water, and let down the nets for a catch."
Luke 5:4

Picture in your mind a roiling sea, beset by storm, as it appears to surrender to a primal chaos and madness. This storm at sea is where our life was cast in our darkest hour. Frightened, we gasp for our last breath. We cannot take flight to escape, for our wings are water soaked. We cannot go up, we can only descend; we are swallowed by the chaos of the deep.

Like a baby in the womb, we have surrendered our need for holy breath. We are sustained by our new environs in the deep. We forget there is freedom on the wing. We are comfortable in our dulled sense of the watery tomb that surrounds us, the only reality we come to know. As we look up, the only sky we can imagine is the blue sea's surface, like what we see when we open our eyes to look up from the bottom of a pool. We dare not dream of the eagle in flight, soaring and circling all the while high above and beyond our imagination.

Then one day, we feel a new sensation, as we are caught up and enmeshed in a Net. We have been in the spiritual fetal position for so long the net easily embraces us like the amniotic sac we see in the medical illustration books. Securely enmeshed, we are tugged upward. Once again our frightened sense of loss of control engulfs us. We struggle to understand as we flip about like a late term baby in the womb, seeking escape. We are in the pangs of rebirth. Jesus, the midwife, waits on shore to breath fresh holy breath into our lungs. We begin to see with new eyes as salt-crusted scales are peeled away; our noses are shocked by the fragrance of the seashore that lies all about us.

As we note in Luke 5:1-11, Jesus was standing by the Lake of Gennesaret with the people crowding around him, listening to the word of God. He saw at the water's edge two boats, left there by the fishermen, who were washing their nets. He got into one of the boats, the one belonging to Simon, and asked him to put out a little from shore. Then he sat down and taught the people from the boat.

When he had finished speaking, he said to Simon, "Put out into deep water, and let down the nets for a catch."

When they had done so, they caught such a large number that their nets began to break. So they signaled their partners in the other boat to come and help them, and they came and filled both boats so full that they began to sink.

Then Jesus said to Simon, "Don't be afraid; from now on you will catch men." So they pulled their boats up on shore, left everything and followed him.

A few years ago I received a call one Saturday morning from the parish answering service. I was the "clergy on call." There was a man named Peter that said he was a parishioner, and that he needed a ride to Catholic Social Services (CSS). He had no car, and no money for a cab. CSS was about a 30-minute drive. He didn't have a phone; he just said he would be standing in front of the Country Market. I was a bit irritated because this was to be my quiet Saturday morning at home. This invasion of peace was an annoyance. But… duty calls… I picked up Peter and drove him to CSS. This was the first of what was to be a regular Saturday Morning gig for probably a year. I got used to it.

Peter was a drug addict and alcoholic. He was fun and engaging, ready to please. Always had a generous smile. He was so pleasant in his slow suicide. I prayed for a way to help him.

Over time, his story came out. I found out he was seven years younger than me, but looked easily 15 or 20 years older than me. One Saturday I remember asking the simple question, "Did you do anything special this week?" "Nothing special. Just went to the park, fell down in the grass, and swallowed a bottle of pills. I am sorry to say, I was ready to die." From his tone, I could tell what he was really sorry about was to still be alive.

Someone found him unconscious and he was resuscitated. The hospital released him the next day.

I finally got the nerve to ask about his past. He had been a "career guy" at Ford, working as an engineer. He had the perfect life, a wife, and his dear four year-old daughter, the apple of his eye. One day he came home and they were gone. Just a note, saying, "Don't bother to look. Too much booze and drugs, no love left." Ten years later, he stopped looking, and settled in our quiet little town to be the town drunk.

We got to CSS, I got out of the car, looked him in the eyes and said, "You know I love you, Peter. If you had killed yourself you would have killed a part of me, too." It was raining, so without much thought, I grabbed from my backseat my umbrella and gave it to him. I had forgotten it had a message on it, "GRACE HAPPENS."

One afternoon the following week I saw him riding a beat up bicycle, umbrella opened and held over his head. I stopped, rolled down my window, and said, "Peter, you look like Mary Poppins. Where you flying off to?" He soberly said, "I got nowhere to go, nowhere to fly off to. You're stuck with me, Deacon!"

Winter rolled around. I suggested that rather than hang out at the Dexter Pub, he should shovel the walks and driveways of the retired folks in town, maybe make a buck here and there. He liked the idea. He started doing just that. One Saturday morning I woke up after a dream. I In it I saw him riding his bicycle, with umbrella over head, as he flew off into the sunrise. He looked back at me, and just giggled. What a joyous feeling I awoke with.

Just before the 5pm Mass, I was vested, praying the rosary with people, kneeling for a moment in prayer. It got really cold out. The temperature dropped to 20 below. Peter came in for Mass. He said he was out shoveling, but that he didn't feel well. He sat down in a pew, collapsed, and died before our eyes. Later, I learned he did all the shoveling expecting no money in return. It was his pleasure to help his elderly neighbors.

It would seem the Lord had a new home for him to fly off to. Just before Mass, he took flight in the shadow of eagle's wings that I'm sure was circling high above us on that wintry windswept day.

There's a peace I've come to know
Though my heart and flesh may fail
There's an anchor for my soul
I can say "It is well"

And I will rise when He calls my name
No more sorrow, no more pain
I will rise on eagles' wings
Before my God fall on my knees
And rise
I will rise[xiv]

Peter, my special saint look down on us. Help us cast our nets into the deep, and be fishers of men. Help us to taste the joy you tasted in Abba's healing forgiveness for sins long ago washed away by the blood of the lamb.

Amen

Day Seven

Intention: To be able to sense the fire of Your infinite love calling me to radiate Your life of charity and service, Lord.

"Lord, I have heard from many about this man,
how much evil he has done to your saints at Jerusalem."
Acts 9:13

The Catholic Church takes sin seriously, but it must do so like Jesus did, by emphasizing God's mercy and trust in the sinner's ability to change, said the preacher of the papal household. "Jesus does not deny that sin and sinners exist," writes Capuchin Father Raniero Cantalamessa. But Jesus "was more severe" toward those who "condemned the sinners than toward the sinners themselves." From scripture we learn, Father Cantalamessa said, "being merciful appears to be an essential aspect of being in 'the image and likeness of God.'" Mercy is the form God's love takes in relation to sinners, he said. "After we have experienced it, we must demonstrate it to our brothers and sisters, both on the level of the church community as well as on a personal level," the Capuchin said.

Now there was a disciple at Damascus named Ananias. The Lord said
to him in a vision, "Ananias." And he said, "Here I am, Lord." And the Lord
said to him, "Rise and go to the street called Straight, and at the house of
Judas look for a man of Tarsus named Saul, for behold, he is praying, and
he has seen in a vision a man named Ananias come in and lay his hands on
him so that he might regain his sight." Acts 9:10-20

How often in our lives is mercy demanded of us? We often have hard feelings towards those we know. A hardness of heart sets in. But Jesus tells us we must show mercy, and he will take care of helping the sinner through the desolation they come to feel. It takes the grace of the Holy Spirit to soften a hard heart. How many of us have had hard feelings for a wrong done by someone we know, and then experienced the liberation of forgiveness, our forgiveness to them. Oh, what a giddy place that takes us to. I praise God every time I search myself and find a hardness I have forgotten about, and go humbly to our Lord to ask for the grace to forgive. That is the moment when we, like Ananias, say, "Here I am, Lord." That is the moment the Signature of Jesus is etched across our heart.

Jesus asks us to consider the healing power of being a forgiving person, even when it feels hard and nearly impossible. But this is demanded of us, if we are to be commissioned to do his will. Let today be an Ananias day, where we see the effects of this grace of forgiveness as it ripples through a Christ-Centered Community. The community that is infused with Eucharist is a warm and welcoming community etched with the Signature of Jesus. That community grows and thrives. May our hearts be etched with the Signature of the Sacred Heart of Jesus. May our lives magnify Christ in the signature that is written on our hearts.

Through our calling,
   May Love sustain,
      May Love provide,
         May Love never cease.

You are God: we praise you;
You are the Lord: we acclaim you;
You are the eternal Father:
All creation worships you.

Come, Lord, help your people.

Intention: To be able to burn with an ardent love in Your promises for new life, Lord.

> *"Blessed are the merciful, for they will be shown mercy.*
> *"Matt 5:7*

God finds us best when we are lost in others.

Mercy is something more than a sentimental, emotional tenderheartedness. The very word mercy is derived from the Latin *"miserum cor"*, a sorrowful heart. Mercy is, therefore, a compassionate understanding of other's unhappiness.

A person is merciful when feeling the sorrow and misery of another as if it were his own. Disliking misery and unhappiness, the merciful person seeks to dispel the misery of his neighbor just as much as he would if the misery were his own. That is why, whenever mercy is confronted not only with pain, but with sin and wrongdoing, it becomes forgiveness which doesn't merely pardon, but ever rebuilds into justice, repentance, and love.

Mercy is compassion that seeks to unburden the sorrows of others as if they were our own. But if we have no compassion, how can compassion come back to us?

Christ has no body but yours,
No hands, no feet on earth but yours,
Yours are the eyes with which he looks
Compassion on this world,
Yours are the feet with which he walks to do good,
Yours are the hands, with which he blesses all the world.
Yours are the hands, yours are the feet,
Yours are the eyes, you are his body.
St Teresa of Avila

If we wish to receive mercy we must be the fiery heart of mercy, for it seems that God finds us best when we are lost in others.

Lesson 3
The Modern Era

Part I
Vatican II and its Impact in Modern Times

Vatican II

The modern era of our Church was ushered in with the winds of change introduced by Vatican II. The ability to hear the Mass in English instead of Latin offered us a chance to actively listen to the Scriptures as never before. It created a growing interest in increasing our understanding and familiarity with Sacred Scripture. With Gospel stories made personal, our hearts were inspired and our lives profoundly moved. In contrast to prior ages, the Church Fathers of Vatican II were inspired to be instrumental in the promotion of this exciting new dawning.

If we were taught anything about Lectio Divina, prior to Vatican II, we were told that it was a special prayer reserved for clergy, religious and monks. In these modern times the Church has called all of the faithful to this "divine reading." It has taken the half century since the encouragement of Vatican II for the movement of Lectio Divina to gain traction.

Pope Benedict and Pope Francis have long been strong proponents of the practice of Lectio Divina. Both stress that this prayer is for all of the faithful. In "Verbum Domini[xv]" Pope Benedict actually described, step by step, how to pray Lectio Divina. A consistent point of emphasis throughout the document is that Christianity must first and foremost offer opportunities for encounters with Jesus Christ.[xvi] As a Jesuit, Pope Francis embraces the practice of Lectio Divina. It has always been an important part of life in the Jesuit community. This Ignatian practice, as we learned in the previous lesson, was created by Ignatius of Loyola, the founder of the Jesuits. Both Popes believe that an encounter with Jesus Christ is necessary for spiritual transformation and the best place to meet Jesus is in the Scriptures.

Impact of Vatican II in the Modern Era

I am a baby boomer. My generation was the grist that fueled the heart of Vatican II reform. Like millions of families in America, my small town Midwestern Catholic family was ambivalent to the changes that swept through our churches. Altar rails got taken away, altars got turned around, statues and side altars disappeared, and the Sunday Missals given to us by our grandparents, became irrelevant. All this left barely a scratch to our collective baby-boomer psyche. Boomers rolled with the punches. In fact I remember the girls in our confirmation class in the late sixties daring to go to Mass without veils. But for our parents and grandparents, these changes were painful. They were not amused by our "sacrilegious" behavior!

My eighth grade teacher, Sister Helene Terese, was the first teacher in our school to take advantage of the movement in the music for the liturgy from Latin to English. I learned to play the guitar, an old upright piano was donated, and the St. Joseph area of the sanctuary became our stage. "No Man Is an Island" was the processional, and "Peace Is Flowing Like a River" substituted the "Lamb of God." The pastor gave in to us, letting us play this music for the School "Low" Mass during the week. This style swept the country, and became known as the "Folk Mass."

Then Sister Helene got us interested in the scripture readings. For me, the notion of being allowed to step in front of the ambo and read scripture was radical. That's when it all began to sink in. Thanks to Sister Helene's mentorship, I finally connected some dots. The family bible that had been reserved for generations as the official record of our family tree actually had the same passages that we read during Mass. Talk about poking a sleeping giant! Sister knew we all had that bible at home, collecting dust. Our assignment was to open them, and find the Mass Readings each week. Our grandparents were concerned we'd scruff up that beautiful, leather bound book that held a place of honor among the knick-knacks on the bookshelf. Oh, the times they were a changin'!

It wasn't until the conclusion of Vatican II in 1965 that the average Catholic in the pew became aware of the notion of bible study. Prior to this Council, expertise in Sacred Scripture was reserved for teachers, preachers and the lettered professorial scripture scholars. In fact, the average Catholic was advised against private study, as it might lead to "heretical" misinterpretation. If questioned, many parish priests would have to admit that in the past they had told their parishioners not to read the Bible. It was simply too "Protestant." The fear was such practice might lead to confusion and division among Catholics. To this day there remain remnants of resistance among Catholics whenever they are encouraged to read the Bible privately or to join a Bible study group.

Of course, Sacred Scripture has always been an important part of Catholic prayer. All of the prayers lovingly memorized and recited, often daily, are steeped in Scripture. Unfortunately, the average Catholic did not recognize their prayers as originating from the words found in the Bible.

Along with the sweeping changes catalyzed by Vatican II, we boomers entered into our rebellious college years; resisting the draft, resisting institutionalization, resisting the authority of our youth, and amazingly waking up Sunday afternoon to find that we weren't struck dead for missing Mass. We inaugurated many movements to support our individual causes, including the sexual revolution of the 60's which led to our acceptance of contraception. We justified our actions with a new phrase Catholics liked, "sensus fidelium," the "sense of the faithful." Collectively we thought of this as the "common sense" of the faithful. If a group of people felt a cause was justified then the "common sense" of the faithful legitimized it. How could it possibly be a sin? This mass rationalization became the measure of our moral bar. This faulty logic was the beginning of the baby boomer generation's slippery slope away from the Church.

In the midst of the sea of change our parents and grandparents always remained steadfast in their Catholic Obligations. So, when we went back home to visit we joined them in their "quaint" traditions to keep the peace, becoming the dreaded Christmas and Easter Catholics. Recognizing this as their only opportunity, the priests, parents and grandparents would shake their finger at us twice a year, casting down dire warnings. Many of us ignored the tirade and simply "fell away" from the Church. For some it was for life, for others like me it was for a decade or two, until a personal crisis served as a wake-up call.

At this point many of us had no mentors to guide us. We became disillusioned with the treadmill of the upwardly mobile "Yuppie" Young Urban Professional generation, with its unfulfilled relationships, secular consumer-oriented media distractions, temporary shared living arrangements, which often led to divorce and annulment. Like many, I landed hard in my thirties and my wake-up call led me to seek a renewed life with the deeper spiritual roots of the Catholic faith as my foundation.

This is where Lectio Divina began to be personal for me. I purchased a bible and a nice zippered covering. I began to discover the treasures within every time I attended Mass and read along with the proclaimed Word of God. Over time, I connected the readings at Mass to reading the Bible. For my journaling, I highlighted and dated any verses that inspired me and changed the highlight color every year. I grew in my faith with a new community of friends. I still have that bible which I look through nostalgically, reading the bookmarks, note cards, and prayer cards given to me by friends and family over the years. As I learned to navigate the bible, I became more than a passive listener to the Word of God. The Holy Spirit makes straight the crooked path, and mends the broken road that leads us back home. Our God is an awesome God!

Part II
Thelma Hall's "Too Deep for Words"[xvii]

In the early 1990's there was little talk about evangelization in the Catholic Church, except in certain apostolic movements, such as Cursillo.[xviii] It was during this period I was introduced to Cursillo through business colleagues and subsequently "lived" my Cursillo at the Salvatorian Center in Methuen Massachusetts. After being raised a "cradle Catholic" I, like many "baby boomers" had a lukewarm attitude about my faith. Cursillo radically changed that for me. I encountered Christ, living and present, which led to a swift and powerful change to my life. From that point on, I wanted fervently to bring others to the Wellspring of Life.

The year following my Cursillo I continued to seek inner spiritual growth. When the opportunity presented itself, I returned to the Center for a Spring Retreat. Providentially, it was on this retreat that I first learned of Lectio Divina. The retreat master had us study and discuss Thelma Hall's book on the topic, "Too Deep for Words." Though it was too complex to absorb in one weekend retreat, it set me on a decades-long journey which continues to this day.

Of particular interest to me was Thelma's description of the method and movements of Lectio Divina, particularly in the area of contemplation. Around that time, there was much being published on the topic of Centering Prayer.[xix] The retreat master warned us of the potential pitfalls and dangers of practicing any form of Centering Prayer not wrapped around Sacred Scripture and the methods of Lectio Divina. To him Lectio Divina was the only path to contemplation worthy of a devout Christian's time. He felt contemplation should always and ever be a drawing into the Sacred Heart of Jesus, the font from which divine mercy flows.

During this era, however, there was a proliferation of methods and techniques of prayer: books, articles, conferences, workshops and such in endless profusion. I spent hours in the local Christian bookstore devouring it all. I, like many at the time, found it all distracting. It was Thelma Hall who pointed out this profusion of methods in her introduction to "Too Deep for Words." To her this was all positive, in that it showed the hunger people had to find meaning and to transcend the mundane reality of everyday life; in essence to satisfy the deepest yearnings of the heart.

As a culture we found ourselves growing pragmatic and restless with our endless "to-do" lists that run out the clock. Yet the heart always desires pathways to inner peace. Thankfully, the Holy Spirit is ever present to inspire leaders to bring us to the bosom of Mother Church. This inspiration finally led to a resurgence of interest in all things contemplative.

The previous chapters outlined the rich history of Lectio Divina and the spiritual splendor it showered on Christianity for centuries. It begs the question, what happened to the promotion of its fruitful practice? Toward the end of the Middle Ages Lectio Divina took a back seat to the teaching of systematized and memorized prayers. By the end of the sixteenth century Church leaders grew fearful that the faithful would misinterpret the reading of Sacred Scripture, given that it was still in Latin. Another fear was of occult practices, especially by everyday parishioners. These fears led to the widespread discouragement of contemplation.

As Thelma Hall explains, "Eventually it came to be generally [erroneously] accepted that contemplation was an extraordinary grace, restricted to an elite few. This was in total contradiction to the traditional teachings of the first fifteen centuries that contemplation is open to all Christians as the normal development of an authentic spiritual life."

It was widely thought that only monks, religious and clergy were availed to the special graces offered through the virtuous practices of Lectio Divina. We know now that it is available to all for spiritual growth. Once we come to taste the living water from the Fountain of Life we are compelled to mission. Mission -- Operatio is developed as the Fifth Movement of Lectio Divina in the final section of this book.

Operatio is being co-missioned by and for Christ. Our mission is to be a witness to His glory because we are all created for union with God.

For Guigo, St John of the Cross, myself and many other, Lectio Divina is a way of life. It is a commitment to lifetime discipleship where we constantly desire to be filled with the good graces of the Sacred Heart of Jesus. By *Praying With the Heart of the Church* we come to realize what it means to follow Christ's example. It is the through our daily prayer of love and presence that we truly come to experience the joy of the Kingdom of God, here and now. Come, taste and see the goodness of the Lord.

Lesson 4
Lectio Divina for the Third Millennium

"If [Lectio Divina] is effectively promoted,
this practice will bring to the Church
a new spiritual springtime."
Pope Benedict XVI

Lectio Divina

Lectio: Read Sacred Scripture

Meditatio: Reflect on the meaning

Oratio: Respond through prayer

Contemplatio: Rest in the Sacred Heart of Jesus

Operatio: Recognize co-mission

<u>Grow:</u> Small Group Study

<u>Go:</u> Personal Call to Action

"...I would like in particular to recall and recommend the ancient tradition of "Lectio Divina": "the diligent reading of Sacred Scripture accompanied by prayer brings about that intimate dialogue in which the person reading hears God who is speaking, and in praying, responds to him with trusting openness of heart" (cf. "Dei Verbum," n. 25). If it is effectively promoted, this practice will bring to the Church — I am convinced of it — a new spiritual springtime." Pope Benedict XVI

Part I
The Four Classic Movements

Lectio: Called to Read Sacred Scripture

The role of Lectio is to facilitate the reunion of a disciple with Jesus as two friends desiring to share time together. The disciple steps toward the Lord because of a desired commitment to Him. Jesus in turn runs to meet him. As with all fruitful interactions between two persons, this exchange results in a deepening and growing relationship.

Lectio involves picking up the Scriptures, invoking the grace of the Holy Spirit, and absorbing the words slowly and thoughtfully. At this point, we must desire to let the words of Scripture sink in and be ingested so that they can nourish the whole person. The careful reading of Scripture becomes the source for prayer for us.

Lectio Divina is indeed reading, but not just ordinary reading. By its very name we see it is Divine Reading which requires active hearing. For reading to become Logos, the Word Made Flesh, we must tune ourselves to the unique way the inspired word harmonizes with our heart, mind and soul. Here, we invoke the Holy Spirit to nurture our mustard seed sized faith and let it grow within us. To be inspired is to breath in deeply, to in-spire the living reality of Logos, the Word Made Flesh.

The Church provides a way to help us prepare. To *Pray with the Heart of the Church* is to choose the Gospel for the upcoming Sunday. Take time to prepare for this awesome gift. Read it slowly, giving it a place of honor in your heart as a gift from God through the Holy Spirit. Quiet your mind and body, and bring your whole person into a single focus. Sit in a way that is most comfortable to you. Be attentive and prepare to be "in-spired."

Being thus prepared and inclined, we become a receptacle for the Holy Spirit to speak within us. We should tune our imaginative faculty to hear more than the mere words leaping from the page by creating an atmosphere of exterior and interior silence. Urge the Spirit. Give yourself freely. Astonishingly, the spirit will lead you to discover something unique, alive and new regardless of the number of times you hear the reading.

Remember the purpose is to discover the living Word that God is speaking today. It is not a strict study method, but an attitude of the heart. Keep an awareness that Lectio Divina is a prayerful encounter with God. Be aware and open to the Holy Spirit with humility and purity of heart.

By letting yourself be drawn to a particular word or phrase, sometimes called the *'shimmering pearl'*, and reflecting on its meaning you are already stepping into the next movement, Meditatio.

Meditatio: Moved to Reflect on the Meaning

Meditatio is the intentional involvement of the mind, probing a deeper understanding of the hidden truth. Here we seek the hidden treasure, the shimmering pearl within Scripture. Guigo described the heart of Lectio Divina as the application of the intellect enlivened by faith. This enlivening results in an increased understanding of the blessed life we are called to live. St. Anselm coined the phrase "Faith seeking understanding." For Anselm, faith seeks understanding, and understanding brings joy. "I pray, O God, to know thee, to love thee, that I may rejoice in thee."

While the role of Lectio is to facilitate the coming together of two friends, in Meditatio our desire is to be drawn to God more deeply. We want to know more about Him, to welcome Him into our lives. We open up to Him as we grow in the virtue of Trust. Through Meditatio, we test the boundaries of who He is, where He is, and what He wants to reveal to us.

Novices to Lectio Divina enter the School of Jesus, where they are exposed to a strange new language, incomprehensible and overwhelming. At this school we write our own dictionary – or rather the Holy Spirit writes it for us – translating His ancient self into our personal humanity. God stands before us in the flesh and blood, the person of Christ Jesus. At the feet of Jesus the Teacher we are taught the language of love. Through the Holy Spirit we gain the wisdom to understand that language and the person of Christ.

Reading in this new language we experience the spiritual reality of "anamnesis" where we recall a past historical event in salvation history, and "epiclesis" where through the power of the Holy Spirit, that event is lifted from the past and brought to our present moment. The power of this face to face encounter compels us to fall in love with Our Lord. At the School of Jesus our hearts burn with desire and we are disposed to converse with him in Prayer.

While discussing Meditatio with a good friend of mine, Kaye, she pointed out that she sees God as an intimate God who yearns for us. Have you really thought of God as yearning for you personally to come close to Him and build a relationship with Him? When Jesus taught us to pray the Our Father, He used the word "Abba" the equivalent of "Daddy." That puts a whole new light on how God wants us to relate to Him. I think we have all had times in our lives where we felt God to be a distant judge. This couldn't be farther from the truth. He IS love, beyond our imagination and deeply wants us to be with Him, resting in His Most Sacred Heart. No matter where we are in our lives, God loves us deeply and yearns for us to open ourselves to His love.

My heart is listening, Lord; open the ears of my heart and say to my soul, I am your salvation. Let me run towards this voice and seize hold of you. Do not hide your face from me: let me die so that I may see it, for not to see it would be death to me indeed. (St Augustine -- Confessions)

Like myself and many others, Kaye read and accumulated knowledge over the years. She experienced some God moments, but didn't truly realize the depth of God's love in her heart until she was in her forties. In varying degrees we all use fear, hurt, justifications, anxiety and inhibitions, baggage which impedes spiritual maturity. Attending a Cursillo Weekend is what helped Kaye realize that God's love was ever present.

The more she intentionally reflected on God's love and presence, the more she engaged all of her senses. Through this she was reminded of her mother's homemade cinnamon rolls. Long before she actually tasted them she would come home, open the door, and be met by the wonderful smell of them baking. If you think about this, I bet you can practically smell them yourself as if they were baking here and now. This is engaging the mental senses. Applying this to meditation means we are part of the passage, picturing ourselves part of the scene and relating it to our life. Through reflection we allow God's word to interact with our thoughts, hopes, memories, and desires so that it touches and affects us at our deepest levels. *"You who walk in the gardens of the scriptures must not cross them either hurriedly or negligently. Dig into each word to draw out its spirit."* (Guerriqued'Igny)

Because He yearns for us God calls us and speaks to us through His Word. We need unbiased openness to the Holy Spirit in order to hear what He is saying to us. We need to let down our guard, set aside our fears. Once we open ourselves to God's presence, we are disposed to accept his call and hear his voice. Thus disposed, we can climb to this next rung of Guigo's ladder, "meditatio," the art of being reflective. This process of engaging in careful thought is the definition of being "reflective."

Take a moment to consider this concept of being reflective. Are you a reflective person? What does this mean? In today's highly stimulated culture, many of us deal with what Ronald Rolheiser calls unbridled restlessness.[xx] This restlessness which has been impressed on us by the culture and environment makes it nearly impossible to be reflective. We need to re-orient and retrain ourselves through practice to intentionally slow down. It is necessary to quiet our mind, seek moments of silence, and rest in the message of His Word. Read, Respond, Reflect and Rest.

We each have unique lives, characteristics, personalities, and environments. Reflecting on the Scriptures gives us perspective – it helps us to see our life in the light of God's Word. It leads to continuous conversion and growth, deepening our relationship with God.

The aim of catechesis is to teach meditation on The Word of God, internalizing it at all times so that it might bear fruit in a new life. (CCC #2688) We reflect on the Word of God to discern what God is revealing to us. We ponder Scripture in relation to our life and its meaning for us today. There is a conversation going on between the reality of our lives and the Word of God. It will tell us truths about God, but also truths about ourselves – both pleasing and challenging.

This concept of meditation was used often by early Church Fathers to describe how we should savor and reflect on God's Word. The image of God's Word "on the palate of the heart" roots deep within us. This process –a "careful repetitious recitation" of the Word, is not meant to be hurried. We listen with the ears of the heart and with the truth of our lives. We then are totally open with all our senses engaged, bringing the truthful reality of our lives in this conversation with God. We are overcome with a sense of wonder and awe in the presence of God.

Oratio: Responding Through Prayer

"Our hearts are restless till they find rest in You"[xxi]

Praying with the Heart of the Church is the devout turning of the heart to God. Once we find the "shimmering pearl" we give thanks to God for gifting it to us. We beg for the grace to be able to live the life that is now a little more profoundly understood. Prayer expresses the personal realization that we can do nothing on our own. We must depend on God's gift of grace. through Jesus' teaching an praying with the heart of the Church, we see that we are not to keep repeating prayer mindlessly like the Pharisees standing at the street corners (Matt 6:5). Rather we recognize that in prayer we express the most important dispositions of the human heart.

The inner rumination, pondering, reflecting in meditatio invites or naturally leads us to speak with God. While reflecting, in meditatio, we have probably had that ah-ha moment or that "wow" or that feeling and knowledge of being given a gift, a gem, an insight. Our natural response is "thank you, God." That, at its simplest, is prayer –dialoguing with God, which is the third step or tool in Lectio Divina: formally called Oratio. Yes, Lectio Divina itself is one big prayer, but in this step we want to go deeper in our prayer – our conversation with God – pertaining to the insights we have just received through reflecting.

I think there is a "borderless border" where Mediatio and Oratio flow and intertwine together. We are already opening ourselves and conversing with God in meditation. The step of Oratio brings this to light more and develops it. We may use words, images, ideas or all three to give to God what we have discovered about ourselves in meditatio. We have experienced God's use of the words, phrase or idea that He has given us as a means of transforming us. This blessing transforms our ideas and memories and we now give to God through prayer what we have newly found within our heart. The entire step of oratio may be further working through of the insight God has given us. With God, we may argue, complain, praise, thank, respond, bargain, petition and surrender – any or all of these – as we talk to God and work through the insights we have been given. Or, our oratio may be as simple as "Thank you for the ah-ha insight."

We have heard and reflected on God's word and now we respond with our words. Teresa of Jesus said, "Prayer is not a lot of thinking but a lot of loving." It is our response to what has been out-poured to us by our God. The early Fathers spoke of four main ways of prayer:

1. *Oratio Compuntionis*: moved to remorse. "Punct" means "pricked". This is an awareness – like a sword piercing our heart that calls us to conversion

2. *Oratio Petitionis:* we see petition in this – an asking for. What do we ask for? The gift of the Holy Spirit – a conversion of heart – a complete openness to God's Will. Help in applying the insights He has given us.

3. *Oratio Eucharistica*: Eucharist means "to give thanks" -- so we have wonder and awe – gratefulness for God's presence and great love.

4. *Oratio laudativa* – this is joyful, spontaneous, and creative; pure praise and worship.

I recently read that prayer can be understood as both a dialogue with God and a consecration. Dialogue because we are having a loving conversation with the One who invites us close to Him, loves and yearns for us. Consecration because we are offering God all parts of ourselves – even those we may have thought in the past He wouldn't want. Through doing this, we allow God's word, which we have received, to touch and change us. God wants us, through prayer, to hold up our difficult and painful experiences to Him and talk to Him over the healing word or phrase He has given us in lectio and meditation. Through this consecration prayer, this giving of ourselves and being totally open to Him, the word of God works to change and heal us. We are opening our real, true selves to His touch.

We have been told to pray always in all circumstances of our lives. As we see God's Word interact with our lives –touch it, change it – so we also bring our lives to God in the light of His Word, through prayer. God calls us family, and he is having a loving talk with us, His children, in hopes of drawing us into that intimate relationship, calling us to rest in the infinite love of His Most Sacred Heart. When we do this, we are in wonder and awe of the loving presence of our God.

Contemplatio: Resting within the Sacred Heart of Jesus

Living the life witnessed in Sacred Scripture is only possible by the mercy of God. Through the anamnesis[xxii] and epiclesis[xxiii] gained in reflection the past is brought into our current moment as an act of the intellect and imaginative facility. If it remains on this intellectual level, it falls short of genuine Prayer. The goal of prayer is not thoughts or concepts or knowledge about Our Lord, but rather the genuine gratitude to God himself as he is, mysteriously hidden in the deepest true self. In the language of the mystics, "God is my me." This Prayer of the Heart is the gateway of the path that leads to the spiritual garden of Contemplatio. We come to prayer spontaneously and naturally as a movement of the heart when we let the Holy Spirit lead us.

The yearning of the heart led us to Lectio Divina. To better understand this yearning lets reflect for a moment on this prayer of St. Augustine:
"Great are You, O Lord, and greatly to be praised; great is Your power, and of Your wisdom there is no end. You have formed us for Yourself, and our hearts are restless till they find rest in You. Lord, teach me to know and understand which of these should be first: to call on You or to praise You or to know You. Those who seek shall find Him, and those who find Him shall praise Him. Let me seek You, Lord, in calling on You, and call on You in believing in You..."

Following in the footsteps of St. Augustine, our inner longing is stirred when we empty ourselves. Through this emptying, we put aside our defenses and masks, and stand before God in our stark need. Over time, we come to realize the restlessness St. Augustine speaks of is itself God longing for us. Oratio is the active effort to keep our hearts open to Him, and to dispose ourselves to the movement of the Holy Spirit. We empty ourselves so that God can fill us with His purpose. Over time, there is less reasoning as the heart takes over in a simple pouring out of love and desire, which takes the form of inner dialogue. As Thelma Hall so aptly states, "Sensing that God is so near and yet so far, the longing of our heart spontaneously calls out to him... begs healing and mercy."

From St Teresa of Avila in her Way of Perfection , we learn that Oratio should be a "prayer of quiet." It is in the quiet that the soul rests in relative peace and senses itself to be closer to God. The desire for union with God becomes stronger. This drives us to be less compulsive. The interior faculties move a bit more spontaneously toward God. Understanding this, we seek to know the Lord, to remember Him alone. And yet another gift of the Holy Spirit strengthens our will as we more resolutely are drawn to him.

For Oratio to move us beyond an intellectual exercise, it cannot be the mere repetition of words. We must engage the deepest part of ourselves. We must come to Him honestly, begging for the grace to remove the obstacles that inhibit direct involvement with Him. Our heart, the very center of our being, is our focus as we envelope ourselves in this movement. A significant goal of Lectio Divina is indeed to recognize and rise above obstacles to a life of grace. These obstacles – our busyness, our anxiety, our competing desires, our fears, our lack of faith, to name a few – are constant temptations to keep us from the joy of the grace poured out to us. We turn in Prayer to God and release these concerns into his hands. The deeper our prayer, the stronger our relationship. In *Oratio* we place ourselves in God's presence, then move on to listening to his word with mind and heart, and finally ask for the grace to be able to respond to him with our whole soul.

This development in *Oratio* opens us to what St Theresa Avila and St John of the Cross considered the ultimate movement of Lectio Divina, *Contemplatio*.

Contemplation is the movement of the mind beyond oneself. It involves experiencing the fruit of *Oratio*. By God's grace we begin to sense from within the life that God invites us to live. St. Theresa of Avila restricted this term, *Contemplatio*, to "special mystical grace from God." Mystical grace is pure gift of the Holy Spirit. Twentieth century theologian Karl Rahner produced volumes of commentary on God, redemption, and the life of grace. Scattered throughout are short and clear statements recognized as seminal insights. One of those statements bears a relationship to what the Christian must strive to be today. *"The Christian of the future will be a mystic or will not exist at all."* Rahner explains in a statement made late in life that mysticism is not some esoteric phenomenon but "a genuine experience of God emerging from the very heart of our existence... The source of spiritual conviction comes not from theology but from the personal experience of God."

Mysticism is being touched by God in a way that is deeper than language, thought, imagination, or feeling. It is knowing God, in Jesus Christ, through the Holy Spirit. He who can pierce our hearts, as His own was pierced. He can lift us beyond any word we might utter. It is as I often say in my reflections on the subject, the movement of the heart "to empty myself of my old self, so that I can be filled with the wisdom to grasp my God-given life purpose. To be an incarnate instrument for the Sacred Heart of Jesus." In short, "to empty myself of myself so that I can become myself." In the words of St Francis Assisi, "*il tuo strumento --make me your instrument.*" St Paul wrote in Acts 17 that it is a personal call. It is "*...to grope for Him and find Him, though He is not far from each one of us; for in Him we live and move and have our being, as even some of your own poets have said, 'For we are His beloved children.'*"

But how is this possible? How do we know something seemingly beyond our grasp, our capacity to speak of it, imagine it, or even clearly feel it? Perhaps a description of my own life-changing experience can be helpful here. As a young boy, I was sitting in church one day in the dark of winter's Christmas solstice. The parish of my childhood was St Patrick Church, a building hand-hewn of stone and timber, a priceless gift from my immigrant forefathers, just a block away from where we lived. I visited it almost daily.

As I sat alone I had what I have come to believe was a mystical experience. In contemplation, in a moment of stark clarity, I was in touch with that which is deepest and most dear to me -- I saw in a transcendent moment something wonderfully present in the physical here and now. In that moment I knew, with words that escaped me, something of Christ's mercy and love for me, melding with my own inner self. It was a life changing moment.

On the subject of mysticism, St. Theresa of Avila wrote that the entire world belongs to God, and he can use small things and situations as means to be present to us. *"Since He is Lord, He is free to do what He wants, and since He loves us, He adapts Himself to our size."*

Mysticism *(Mystical Union)* is the memory of first love, of God's kiss as he knitted us, body and soul, into our mother's womb. It is that moment of stark clarity where our spiritual senses are defined and enlivened. Thomas Merton call it the *Pointe Verge*[xxiv]. It is a point of pure truth where we come to realize that which is deepest and most dear, the framework of reality itself. In that clarity, one knows what one must do, as opposed to what one's intellect might think it wants to do.

What then, is our deepest mystical memory? Mystical union, truth, goodness, and beauty inside the human soul. Henri Nouwen called it *"first love, the distant memory of once having been loved and caressed by hands far gentler than any we have ever met in this world; the barely conscious memory of having been with God before we were born."*

Most of us don't have a name for this memory, but we speak of experiences as "ringing true" or "not ringing true." Do we carry some kind of GPS inside of us that guides us home? I believe we do. It is a hearkening from within the deepest center of our being. We know that we are urged to return to that mystical far country. We touch in our most sincere moments that place where we are branded by first principles -- the feel of God's gossamer kiss across our cheek. Of this we are certain. We must be true to who we are, beloved children of our God.

To hearken to His call, to live our days as disciples of Christ, that is our destiny. To respond intentionally to the nudges and urges of the Holy Spirit. Indeed, we "live and move and have our being"

(Acts 17:28) in small steps toward the New Jerusalem our living the mystically-driven life.

In the three prior successive movements, Lectio, Meditatio, and Oratio, we are directed toward a greater depth, yet we are still in the mental realm of our own dominating activity. The transition to Contemplatio is very unlike what one might have expected. For while we are moving toward God who is Light, our path becomes dark and obscure.

God infuses us as we close down our natural facilities of reason and imagination. Thinking and reasoning about God ceases within us. What I have discovered in my years of spiritual direction is that this is frequently confused with desolation, where our desire for devotion dries up. It is here that we wander in the ultimate desert experience, and are tempted to give it all up. But we must have the resolve to believe that we are on the threshold of His beautiful and bountiful Garden. In his writings on Contemplatio, St. John of the Cross says *"it is nothing else than a secret and peaceful and loving inflow of God, which, if not hampered, fires the soul in the spirit of love."*

In Contemplatio we learn silence, and not to do but simply be. Contemplation is the place where our thoughts and concepts, imagination, senses and feelings are abandoned for a faith that dwells in what is unseen and unfelt. We learn here, often in a painful and stark way, that the image of God and Heaven constructed across our lifetime falls like a house of cards and we are left in a "cloud of unknowing"[xxv] where God is unseen and unfelt and seemingly absent to our senses. Yet, we are with patience and trust infused with the sure wisdom that in this stark desert somehow He is in fact present; and in this silence is His speech. It is in entering the unknown, letting go of everything familiar, and discovering that in being "wretchedly and pitiably poor and blind and naked, too" (Rev 3:17) lies the potential to bathe in the River of Life, the font of Love and Joy.

The superficial self is an illusion, and we must shed it if we are to "lighten up" for our ascending journey. It is this false self that strives to possess that which we cannot hold, that which can never be grasped because wisdom is a gift, to be received with open hands and heart.

Pope Benedict XVI states in his encyclical "God is Love: Deus Caritas Est," "'God is love, and he who abides in love abides in God, and God abides in him' (1 Jn 4:16). These words from the First Letter of John express with remarkable clarity the heart of the Christian faith: the Christian image of God and the resulting image of mankind and its destiny. In the same verse, Saint John also offers a kind of summary of the Christian life: 'We have come to know and to believe in the love God has for us'." It is our selfish impulses that want to know that which cannot be known. It is from God's font of pure love that we are illuminated in the "unknowning" and gain the wisdom of pure "*agape*" love.

When we struggle to preserve autonomy, control, and being the center of our own meaning, we fail to navigate the darkness. St John of the Cross believed that this darkness and seeming desolation is in fact a gift of God's compassion. In this darkness we experience the beginning of Contemplation.

Thomas Merton expands on this concept of darkness in his Night of the Senses:

"The life of infused contemplation does not always begin with a definite experience of God in a strong in-pouring of light. Moments of freedom and escape from the blindness and helplessness of the ordinary, laborious ways of the spirit will always be relatively rare. And it is not too hard to recognize these sudden, intense flashes of understanding, these vivid "rays of darkness" striking deep into the soul and changing the course of a man's whole life. They bring with them their own conviction. They strike blindness from our eyes like scales. They plant in us too deep and too calm and too new a certainty to be misunderstood or quickly forgotten." [xxvi]

For both John of the Cross and Merton, one's lifetime is a series of false constructs that can bring us to disappointment and sorrow. When we move from one level of spiritual maturity to the next, the false constructs collapse, potentially leaving us in the darkness they so well explain. But, trusting in God's providential care is the point of surrender to the darkness, where God can then liberate us from illusion.

Merton further expands on this concept:

"The mind finds itself entering uneasily into the shadows of a strange and silent night. The night is peaceful enough. But it is very frustrating. Thought becomes cramped and difficult. There is a peculiarly heavy sense of weariness and distaste for mental and spiritual activity. Yet at the same time the soul is haunted with a fear that this new impotence is a sin, or a sign of imperfection. It tries to force acts of thought and will. Sometimes it makes a mad effort to squeeze some feeling of fervor out of itself, which is, incidentally, the worst thing it could possibly do. Ah the pretty images and concepts of God that it once cherished have vanished or have turned into unpleasant and frightening distortions. God is nowhere to be found. The words of prayers return in a hollow echo from the walls of this dead cave.

If a man in this night lets his spirit get carried away with fear or impatience and anxiety, he will come to a standstill. And finally he will run away from darkness, and do the best he can to dope himself with the first light that comes along.

But there are others who, no matter how much they suffer perplexity and uneasiness in the wilderness where God begins to lead them, still feel drawn farther and farther on into the wasteland. They cannot think, they cannot meditate. Their life of prayer is without light and without pleasure and without any feeling of devotion.

On the other hand they sense, by a kind of instinct, that peace lies in the heart of this darkness. Something prompts them to keep still, to trust in God, to be quiet and listen for His voice; to be patient and not to get excited. Soon they discover that all useless attempts to meditate only upset and disturb them; but at the same time, when they stay quiet in the muteness of naked truth, resting in a simple and open-eyed awareness, attentive to the darkness which baffles them, a subtle and indefinable peace begins to seep into their souls and occupies them with a deep and inexplicable satisfaction. This satisfaction is tenuous and dark. It cannot be grasped or identified. It slips out of focus and gets away. Yet it is there."

Perhaps nothing more simple and basic may be said about Contemplatio than that it is the acceptance of God's invitation to entrust one's self totally to Him, so that he may lift us beyond ourselves. In St. Augustine's view, we are born to Original Sin, to "cupidity", that prideful, selfish, self-absorbed, idolatrous self. In Contemplatio we enter into that mysterious journey into His pure love, where our soul is fired in the spirit of love. It is in this resting garden, "abiding in Thee" that the Spirit of Jesus may pray in us and love in us.

Abide in Thee! 'tis thus I only know
The secrets of Thy mind even while below—
All joy and peace, and knowledge of Thy word,
All power and fruit, and service for the Lord.

Part II
The Fifth Movement Operatio: Go Out to the World

A New Spiritual Springtime

Lifetime Discipleship:

The concept of Lifetime Discipleship is a hot topic in the Church today. In Advent of 2011, Bishop Earl Boyea, our bishop here in the diocese of Lansing, promulgated his pastoral letter, *"Feed My Sheep: A Vision for Evangelization, Engagement and Discipleship"*[xxvii] In this document, he calls the faithful in his diocese to set evangelization, engagement and discipleship as a top priority for the diocese and parishes, to ensure that the mission of the Church of Lansing is to bring all people to Christ through the Church.

Conversion of the heart is essential and must inform all preaching in our churches. The call of Jesus was to a radical discipleship, which changed every aspect of life. As St. Paul tells us, *"we no longer live for ourselves, but for him."* Jesus invites us to daily deny ourselves, take up our cross and follow him. Catholic preachers must live out their promise to:

> *"...believe what they read, teach what they believe, and practice what they teach."*

If they do so, they will be able to invite others to:

> *"Be imitators of me, as I am of Christ." (I Cor 11:1)*

Lifetime Discipleship, then, is the ongoing transformation of each of us following an authentic encounter with Christ, where we progressively become like Jesus in character and purpose as we grow in intimacy with him.

Operatio:
Recognizing what it means to be Co-Mission with Christ

How can we take care that no impure thoughts pass the boundaries set by our Holy Fathers? We must study and be righteously taught. We know it does not help us to ignore what is seen through meditation. How can we not respond with what we know we must do? Through the help of prayer and God's grace we are charged to hold what is found in reflection, and understand what must be done for the soul's health. The Apostle James says: ' Every good and perfect gift is from above, coming down from the Father of the heavenly lights, a Father who does not change like shifting shadows. '(James 1:17) Without his help and heavenly grace we are unable to do any good.

What, then, does the Church offer as a follow up to an individual's "encounter with Christ"? There have been many solutions offered over the years. But perhaps the most enduring is the Cursillo model of the "Fourth Day". The Fourth Day is essentially every day of the rest of your life, as you complete "living" your Cursillo Weekend.

Jackie Rowe, a fellow Cursillista and friend, has this to say about the Fourth Day, as taught to Cursillistas here in the Diocese of Lansing (DOL):

The DOL Fourth Day includes the offering for group and community faith sharing with like-minded Christians on a weekly basis. As much as this is planned for those who have lived their Cursillo Weekend, some people may receive encouragement to live the weekend by attending "Reunion Group" or "Ultreya" before actually "living" their weekend.

A candidate for the Cursillo Weekend will learn about the "Fourth Day" offered at local parishes, through talks given and follow-up discussion while attending the Weekend. This should be shared as an "offering" -- not as something that has to be continued, but rather, something that the Cursillo Team endeavors to inspire as a desire for the Weekend Candidate. Following the Weekend, the sponsor takes the responsibility to invite the new Cursillista to sharing the Reunion Group experience. This invitation is a way to assure local parish follow up.

Nationally, this is the tradition that follows the "essence" of Cursillo. The formation and standards they hold are in sync with the founder of the Cursillo Movement, Eduardo Bonin, whose philosophy and plan urges that every Cursillista belong to a lifetime discipleship group. The Lansing Diocese Cursillo plan follows this essence as much as possible, however, adaptation for local differences have been accommodated, so that all areas of the diocese adapt to the needs of local Cursillistas. New Centers in the Lansing Diocese emerge as the numbers of Cursillistas increase and are ready to begin a Reunion Group.

For some areas of the diocese, there are small reunion groups with men and women meeting separately at different times. Others may have chosen to group with men and women together - because of the numbers of Cursillistas they have or because their Reunion Group has evolved into a faith-filled sharing each member grows from. Some Cursillistas have returned home from their weekend to a Faith/Prayer group they were involved with pre-Cursillo, sharing their newfound knowledge of Cursillo with them. All of these groups exist as they are led through the urging of the Holy Spirit in leading them.

In other words, Cursillo has for its members the weekly "Small Group Reunion" where a few people gather weekly for prayer, study, and a sharing by each individual of their calling in the mission field. (i.e. where has Christ been encountered in the face of others in the community) This has proved to be a sustainable model over the years.

If you wish to learn more about the Cursillo Movement, I encourage you to visit http://lansingcursillo.org

Grow and Go

- *Grow Christian growth through a Small Group of Lifetime Disciples*

- *Go follow one's personal call to action as a disciple*

Grow through Small Christian Groups:

Using the Cursillo model of the local parish Group Reunion, lifetime discipleship is centered in the life of a local church, where the fellowship of other disciples encourage, teach, and safeguard the believer's discipleship process (see Heb. 10:24-25).

As small groups form, individuals experience over time, through "Habitus", ongoing transformation, where the heart is emptied of self-serving desires, and is filled with the Sacred Heart of Jesus, in character and purpose, for the incarnate outpouring of divine love.

What is this "Habitus"? Think of it as spiritual fortitude. Fortitude as an incarnate gift of the Holy Spirit, exists best where two or more gather on a regular (usually weekly) basis.

The power of fortitude is communally created and constantly re-legitimized through the interplay of grace and structure. The main way this happens is through 'habitus,' defined as group norms or tendencies that guide behavior and thinking. Habitus is the way group synthesis becomes forged in individuals in the form of lasting dispositions that eventually move from the conscious decision process to the subconscious, which then guide them. The structure recommended in this book is achieved when we *Grow* Christian communities through Small Groups of Lifetime Disciples, following the heart and mind of the Church through lectionary-based Lectio Divina.

Habitus is a group reality, rather than an individual, which lead to patterns that are enduring and transferrable from one part of life to another, but that also dynamically shift and grow in relation to specific contexts and over time.

Habitus is neither a result solely of free will, nor determined by structures, but created by a kind of interplay between structure and the individual's commitment to intentionally live out the Gospel message over time (i.e. to <u>Go</u>) These life changes and spiritual dispositions are both shaped by the encounter with Christ, and the structures of the small group, that shape the current practices of the individual within their environment to be "leven" in the marketplace.

This journey usually comes about following a radical and intimate encounter with Jesus Christ. Within the encounter, one is given, through the Holy Spirit, a lived reality of reconciliation and conversion, from our sinful self, to love for Christ and others. This usually happens within the context of a multiple-day retreat in prayer and study. (see Matt. 5:48; Eph. 4:13-15; Phil. 2:5)

Lifetime discipleship, through "Habitus", suffuses every dimension of life and is progressive in nature. It is not merely obedience to the 10 Commandments, it follows Christ's command, "I tell you, unless your righteousness surpasses that of the scribes and Pharisees, you will not enter into the kingdom of heaven." (see Matt 5:20) For many, following their radical conversion, they look for progressive growth throughout the year. When growth in intimacy with Christ dries up, the once-healthy relationship seems to diminish. (see John 15:4). Those who follow Jesus' life and teaching will be prepared to eagerly share their faith experiences and to invest themselves in the spiritual nurture of others (see Matt. 28:18-20; 2 Tim. 2:2).

<u>Go</u> live your Mission:

It is the Holy Spirit who transforms life and cannot be initiated through the effort of any individual who merely tries to be good. As Guigo the Carthusian explained, it is, and can only be, a work of actualized, cooperative grace. While God transforms, a believer's spiritual practice creates the transforming environment in which the Holy Spirit works (see Phil. 2:13; 1 Tim. 4: 7-8).

Christian discipleship always manifests itself in ministry to others (Go live your mission). Every Christian has been spiritually gifted for the purpose of service (see 1 Pet. 4:10).

Sample Lectio Four Part Series:

 GROW † GO

Week 1:   Grow: Orientation and Lectio

Worship Space:

6:30 pm	Solemn Evening Prayer	
6:50 pm	Introduction, Welcome, Intro	Pastoral Associate
6:55 pm	Presentation I Orientation and Lectio	Pastor

Parish Hall:

7:30 pm	Small Groups break out	Team
8:10 pm	Q/A from groups to presenter	
8:25 pm	Closing prayer	Pastor

Week 2:   Grow: Meditatio and Oratio

Worship Space:

6:30 pm	Solemn Evening Prayer	
6:50 pm	Welcome	Pastoral Associate
6:55 pm	Presentation II Meditatio and Oratio	Pastoral Associate

Parish Hall:

7:30 pm	Small Groups break out	Team
8:10 pm	Q/A from groups to presenter	
8:25 pm	Closing prayer	Priest/Deacon

Week 3:   Grow: Contemplatio

Worship Space:

6:30 pm	Opening Song	
6:40 pm	Welcome	Pastoral Associate
6:45 pm	Presentation III Contemplatio	Guest Speaker
7:30 pm	Break	
7:45 pm	Exposition/Night Prayer	Priest/Deacon
8:20 pm	Benediction/Reposition	Priest/Deacon

Week 4:   Go: Operatio

Worship Space:

6:30 pm	Solemn Evening Prayer	
6:50 pm	Welcome	Pastoral Associate
6:55 pm	Presentation IV Operatio	Youth Leader

Parish Hall:

7:30 pm	Small Groups break out	Team
8:10 pm	Q/A from groups to presenter	
8:25 pm	Closing prayer	Priest/Deacon

Lifetime Discipleship:
Engagement of the Small Basic Christian (SBC) Group
In Lectionary-based Lectio Divina

GROW + GO

"Mystery, adventure, self discovery, melding with the very substances of people's lives produce shimmering pearls of wisdom from Lectio Divina. Forming Small Groups at the local parish level over time lead to personal spiritual growth."

Guidelines for New SBC Groups:

New small groups need guidance during the formative period. Parish leadership should promote formation of small groups. A series of talks on lectionary-based Lectio Divina, for example, could be organized after weekend Masses, or during the week. *(see chart)* One rotating member of the group could be assigned each week, prepared to bring a short reflection on the upcoming Sunday's Gospel. This reflection should first be an exegesis that describes the literal sense of the scripture. Most of this exegesis will be available in the Liturgical Calendar Companion, available with this book.

The facilitator should encourage the members of the group to lay out, over time, their life story at the service of the Holy Spirit and the Sacred Scriptures. The Holy Spirit then mingles personal stories and Scripture that speak personally to each member. The Word comes alive and becomes relevant.

During this process this leader should introduce the members to the many qualified sources available in the parish library. The leader should foster in the group an attitude to be open and docile to the Holy Spirit.

The pastor, spiritual directors and table leaders, understanding the stories of the people, are then able to help the group hear what the Spirit is trying to say. He or she should reflect back to the group and the group should reflect to the leader. Hence, wonder and awe moments are fostered during this process. Over time each member comes to better discern their purpose in life, prepared and equipped with mission and passion in the world.

Lectio Divina

Lectio:	The Art of Listening
Meditatio:	The Art of Reflection
Oratio:	The Art of Prayer from a Grateful Heart
Contemplatio:	The Art of Self-Emptying
Operatio:	The Art of Ministry

<u>Grow:</u> Spiritual Maturity

<u>Go:</u> ...to the Mission Field

Let the word of Christ dwell in you richly, teaching and admonishing one another in all wisdom, singing psalms and hymns and spiritual songs, with thankfulness in your hearts to God. Colossians 3:15-16

In conclusion, I remind you that Lectio Divina is a practice rarely perfected overnight. I have been practicing this art since 1990, and am still struck with wonder and awe at the daily joyful encounter of Christ, thanks to these holy movements.

We are spiritually free when our spiritual and emotional being experiences joy. Lectio Divina leads us daily to joyful passion leading to a faithful, hopeful and loving life. I encourage you to give this gift to yourself and pray daily with the heart of the Church. Let the Spirit of the Lord dwell in you richly. May Lectio Divina lead you not only to balance and well being, but to the astonishing realization that Christ is the light of the world. And may He, the source of all mercy, lead you, your family and friends, and community to a renewed spiritual springtime!

References

[i] Synoptic meaning similar; syn – one, optic – lense. seeing through one lens

[ii] Excerpt from the Catechism of the Catholic Church 2652-2654

[iii] Barakah: Ancient Jewish word for "Small Blessings"; See John 6:3-14 Jesus blesses the loaves given by the boy; Barakah prayer typically begins with, "Blessed are you, Lord God of All Creation..." and ends with "Blessed be God forever!" or similar.

[iv] Feast of Booths John 7:1-52

[v] See the Anti-Pelagian Writings of St Augustine

[vi] see St Augustine's 'Enchidrion'

[vii] Hymn: Ubi Caritas, tr. Omer Westendorf (1961) Tune: Christian Love, CM, by Paul Benoit (1961).

[viii] A lover of wine

[ix] Carmelite Constitutions (No. 82)

[x] Meditations from St John of the Cross; Imago Dei Christian Community; copyright 2017, imagodeocommunity.ca

[xi] A poem by St John of the Cross (died 1591), Translated from the original Basque by Rev. David Rosenberg in 2005, with the assistance of students of classical studies; Department of Classical Studies; University of Michigan, Ann Arbor, Michigan

[xii] Finding God in All Things: A Marquette Prayer Book © 2009 Marquette University Press

[xiii] by Luc Olivier Merson, copyright 2003, used by permission

[xiv] words from the song I Will Rise by Chris Tomlin, copyright protected

[xv] Verbum Domini is a post-synodal apostolic exhortation issued by Pope Benedict XVI in 2010 which deals with how the Catholic church should approach the Bible.

[xvi] Olson, Carl E. - OSV Newsweekly, 12/12/2010

[xvi] Too Deep for Words; Thelma Hall, RC; Paulist Press; Copyright 1988 by Cenacle of St. Regis

[xviii] Cursillo Movement: for more information visit www.lansingcursillo.org

[xix] For arguments against classical Centering Prayer, you are encouraged to navigate to: https://www.catholic.com/magazine/print-edition/the-danger-of-centering-prayer

[xx] for more on this topic read "Shattered Lantern"; Ronald Rolheiser;

[xxi] Confessions; St Augustine

[xxii] Anamnesis -- recalling and bringing alive a past historical event

[xxiii] Epiclesis -- a past historical event is lifted from the past and brought to our present moment through invoking the power of the Holy Spirit

[xxiv] Pointe Verge; Thomas Merton; Seeds of Contemplation; A point of nothingness; a point of pure truth.

[xxv] Cloud of Unknowing -- a Spiritual Guide to Contemplative Prayer; Author: a late 14th century Christian Mystic written in Middle English;

[xxvi] New Seeds of Contemplation; Thomas Merton; New Directions Publishing; Copyright 1961 by the Abbey of Gethsemani, Inc.

[xxvii] Feed My Sheep: A Vision for Evangelization, Engagement and Discipleship; Most Rev. Earl Boyea, Diocese of Lansing; Faith Catholic Publishing 2011